David W. Hkos

Exponential Technologies

D0882337

Exponential Technologies

Higher Education in an
Era of Serial Disruptions

Darrel W. Staat

ROWMAN & LITTLEFIELD
Lanham • Boulder • New York • London

Published by Rowman & Littlefield
An imprint of The Rowman & Littlefield Publishing Group, Inc.
4501 Forbes Boulevard, Suite 200, Lanham, Maryland 20706
www.rowman.com

6 Tinworth Street, London SE11 5AL, United Kingdom

British Library Cataloguing in Publication Information Available

Library of Congress Cataloging-in-Publication Data
Names: Staat, Darrel W., 1941– author.
Title: Exponential technologies : higher education in an era of serial
  disruptions / Darrel W. Staat.
Description: Lanham, Maryland : Rowman & Littlefield, 2019. | Includes
  bibliographical references.
Identifiers: LCCN 2018046229 (print) | LCCN 2018060010 (ebook) | ISBN
  9781475848618 (Electronic) | ISBN 9781475848595 (cloth : alk. paper) |
  ISBN 9781475848601 (pbk. : alk. paper)
Subjects: LCSH: Education, Higher—Effect of technological innovations on.
Classification: LCC LB2395.7 (ebook) | LCC LB2395.7 .S76 2019 (print) |
DDC
  371.33/44678—23
LC record available at https://lccn.loc.gov/2018046229

♾™ The paper used in this publication meets the minimum requirements
of American National Standard for Information Sciences—Permanence
of Paper for Printed Library Materials, ANSI/NISO Z39.48-1992.

Printed in the United States of America

Contents

Preface

"Forewarned, forearmed."

—Anon.

The twenty-first century is here. There is no going back. The first decade of the new century slammed the door on what came before. It is time to kiss the past goodbye. Business as usual is about to change dramatically. The first decades of the twenty-first century are unveiling a number of developing technologies that will impact higher education, business, society, and culture far beyond any changes experienced in the history of mankind.

The world is caught in the beginnings of a digital flow that is phenomenally rapid, unpredictable, and frightening. Fortunately, the technological developments can be somewhat predictable if we begin to understand them. Awareness can make all the difference.

So what is coming? To begin, it is important to understand what is going. The gradual, predictable, linear patterns of life and work experienced in the twentieth century about to slip away without much explanation, fanfare, or warning. The life and work currently accepted as normal has begun to morph into ever-changing technological configurations that seem to appear from nowhere.

The world is beginning to slide toward an era of serial disruptions. What was normal in the past will evaporate like mist in the morning sun as technologies invade transportation, manufacturing, genome modification, and the definition of intelligence, to name a few.

Never before have we seen a point in time where virtually every single industry was being disrupted. The disruption of every industry is also causing a bit of unrest as people struggle to define where they fit or if they will become obsolete. It's forcing us to adapt and change to stay relevant while giving rise to new business models, new products, new companies, new behaviors, and new ways of simply existing in today's world. (Morgan, 2014, p. 19)

The Fourth Industrial Revolution is upon us (Schwab, 2016). On many fronts, the human mind is creating a technological world that will totally transform work, life, society, and culture. Attempts to explain how this happened or what to do about it using twentieth-century models will not provide much help in understanding it. Those models provide linear thinking, where things happen one day at a time in a foreseeable manner. Human beings are able to adapt to linear changes in a relatively easy manner. What is in front of us with the ten technologies described in this book is totally different.

The new technologies are not merely another automobile, phone, or aircraft. Instead, the digital age brings new technologies into existence at first quite gradually so that they look to be developing in a linear manner. The difference is that they develop that way only for a time before they shift to an exponential velocity that makes them difficult to understand, adapt to, or accept.

The twenty-first century will not only be a time of transforming changes on many fronts, but also the changes will develop at lightning speed that will make learning how to deal with them most difficult. Most difficult, that is, if we are not aware of their presence, are ignoring their potential impact, or are unprepared to deal with them. Should we be afraid? Only if we are not aware and unprepared. Becoming aware and preparing to deal with the technologies are the focus of this book.

In the world of community colleges and universities, was there anything in the past that might be of assistance to help us to face the new future? Perhaps one. Looking back to the 1980s, when the personal computer came into existence, prognosticators feared that the computer would replace clerical workers. It was thought that the computer would literally take over the work of the secretary. Those employed in clerical positions were cautioned that they should begin looking for work elsewhere.

During that decade, did the clerical staff at the institutions of higher education and business disappear? No, they did not. If fact, they became more important than they had been previously. New activities, new processes, and new ways of thinking arrived on the scene that were not foreseen when the technology became available, which helped the institutions of higher education and businesses become more effective and efficient than they had ever been in the past.

What was observed in higher education during the decade of the 1980s was that the clerical staff learned new skills to successfully use computers, which developed considerably more data rapidly, all of which helped to improve the institution. The administration began to make decisions based on current data rather than last semester's or last year's information, good guesses, or gut feelings. The entire institution developed along new pathways.

Faculty soon brought the computer to the classroom and lab. Typewriters went out the door to be replaced first by word processors and then by PCs. It happened in a period of two to three years. The computer impacted program offerings as well. In the community college, the Secretarial Science program became the Administrative Assistant program. Use of the computer completely changed the role of the secretary to that of the assistant at the educational institution and in the business community. Lengthy printouts of information became spreadsheets printed on sheets of 8.5 × 11 paper.

By the end of the twentieth century, almost every program offered in a community college or university used the computer extensively. The business community who hired the graduates demanded the change to the use of computers as they had to competitively deal with national and international businesses. By the end of the century, the computer and the Internet created a global economy that continues to grow and develop.

The twenty-first century is another phenomenon altogether. In its first 18 years, the technology of Narrow Artificial Intelligence, autonomous cars, drones, 3-D printing, personal robots with human features, the Internet of Things with sensors continuously reporting to the cloud, and genome development with CRISPER/Cas9, are no longer science fiction ideas, but realities developing at what was appears to be a normal, linear rate.

However, do not be lulled into complacency. These and more technologies in the wings are preparing to enter the global environment at an exponential rate of speed. They will disrupt current processes and will have to be dealt with. They will provide more efficient and effective ways of doing things, which will benefit the higher education and the business world.

As the founding president York County Technical College, I made many visits to manufacturing businesses in the county to ascertain how the college might support them with training. One company in particular stood out. It manufactured electronic products. The CEO of that firm said their products went from an idea to development to manufacturing to sales to obsolescence in nine months. Products went from concept to deletion in a mere nine months.

In order to make that time frame work, he told me that they were continuously researching what they thought would be needed, conferring with potential customers, and taking advantage of what the data demonstrated would be needed. The company flourished. Their method of accurately predicting the future needs in their industry worked.

The process that company used to develop products from idea to obsolescence in nine months might serve as a model for business in the twenty-first century (Ismail, 2014). Why? Because that kind of speed, perhaps more, will be necessary to keep up with technological developments in the very near future.

What about higher education? Could the nine-month pattern work there as well? Unfortunately, there will not be a choice. Speed will win out. Not only will a nine-month process be needed, but more than likely a six-month method as well, and maybe even less. It will bring a topsy-turvy world as a brutal reality to the educational environment.

The exponential change will require new thinking on how to pursue the path that leads to success. It will be a game changer for all concerned. Community colleges and universities will need to be at the front edge of the methods needed to deal with the exponentially developing technologies.

Learning to unlearn and relearn will become the mantra of business and industry in the near future as technologies develop exponentially. Sustainability and success will demand a mindset of continual, rapid, ever-changing growth. The digital paradigm of the twenty-first century will require new ways of thinking, working, and living. Continual education of the workforce will no longer be a nice to have, but will become the requirement for success.

Community colleges and universities will not be able to stand on the sidelines observing what is happening to the business world. They will have to jump into the maelstrom, working shoulder to shoulder with the business world. There will be little choice to do otherwise. Those who do not take the jump into the seeming chaos will soon find themselves, their institutions, faculty, and staff without students. Those who jump in the fray will realize that leading and operating an institution of higher education will take new, ever-changing skills and abilities to remain viable and successful for all concerned.

Unreasonable as it may seem to those in the worlds of business and in higher education, the velocity of change created by technologies will impact both areas causing a new paradigm of how to operate successfully in an exponential environment. The goal of this book is to assist the administrators, faculty, and staff in community colleges and universities to develop the understanding and future-focused thinking needed to keep institutions of higher education viable, worthwhile, and successful by serving the business community with the digital tools and a technologically trained workforce.

A word of caution. Some readers may find this book not to their liking. Some may want to interpret it as "the sky is falling" nonsense. Others may find the text frightening and turn away to ignore the world that seems to be appearing. However, others will embrace the notions discussed and make an effort to use the guidance given.

Whatever the reaction, remember this: the technologies discussed and described in this book exist and are currently developing. They are coming, like it or not. To be forewarned is to be forearmed.

Acknowledgments

I want to thank my colleagues at Wingate University who provided interest and support for my research into technology and its impact on community colleges and universities.

I want to thank Dr. Annette Digby, Dean of the Thayer School of Education, for her continual support and encouragement. She is an inspiration to whom I owe much.

Finally, I greatly appreciate the love and concern of my wife, Beverly, who is patient with the many hours I spend in my home office researching and writing.

Introduction

It is critical that community college and university administrators and faculty become aware of the impending impact of a series of technologies on their institutions that are developing in the twenty-first century. Look back about ten years. Uber did not exist. Airbnb did not exist. If one wanted to a ride home from the airport, a phone call to a taxi company was needed. If a person was traveling to another state and city, a phone call to a motel would be made for a reservation.

What about today? Those two options are still available; however, others, usually less expensive, are open to the consumer as well. Uber or Lyft can be contacted for the ride home from the airport. The trip away from home can use Airbnb to locate a room for the night. Most interesting is that today Uber transports more customers than the traditional taxis. Airbnb has more rooms than all the hotels and motels in the United States put together. How did that happen? How did that happen so fast? The answers to those questions go back to becoming aware, which is critical; however, it is not nearly enough, as will be seen later.

Community colleges and universities will need to make significant changes in how they deal with students, programs, instruction, equipment, technology, and facilities The time of the appearance of calm normality, which describes the initial stage of the development of the twenty-first technologies, will literally disappear as the technologies reach the exponential stage and grow like unforeseen tsunamis appearing without warning from nowhere.

SERIAL DISRUPTIONS

If there was only one technology developing at a time, it might be handled somewhat reasonably. However, since there are a series of technologies developing, many will reach the exponential stage in close proximity to each other. That will create the era of serial disruptions intruding upon the scene. Reacting to serial disruptions will require a revised method of thinking and acting. That revised method will become a new paradigm to deal with the rapid, continuous development of technologies that will affect community colleges and universities.

The community college with its focus on practical job training will be impacted as the business community accepts and uses the technologies. Since most every business exists as part of a global economy, each will have to keep up with the latest in technological development in order to compete in the international marketplace. If the community college is to remain successful in the technology world of the twenty-first century, it will have to make significant changes in how it operates.

Universities, as well, will soon find themselves drawn into the need for serious change. The business community will be looking to them for guidance and development of various segments of the technologies that are most useful to them. That assistance may come in the form of algorithms, software, and products. To top it off, elementary and secondary education will not be far behind as they prepare the young people to enter higher education.

PREPARING FOR
EXPONENTIAL DEVELOPMENT

This book attempts to assist leaders in community colleges and universities become aware of what is coming, and suggest what can be done to deal with technologies that are about to grow at exponential rates. The new paradigm will require that the current linear practice of administration transform into an exponential method of leadership. Preparing for the paradigm will demand serious revisions of operation for successful higher education on the part of administrators, faculty, staff, and board members.

It should be remembered as one reads through the chapters of this book that technologies are man-made attempts to create a better world for all. No matter whether that is a clothes washer, refrigerator, automobile, boat, personal computer, cell phone, battery-powered lawn mower, and hundreds of other products that are daily taken for granted, they exist because there is a market for them. So it is with the technologies discussed on the pages of this book.

My grandparents farmed on the plains of South Dakota. On Mondays my grandmother heated the water in a stove that burned corn cobs. She carried the hot water from one shed to the building that held the clothes washer. She operated the washer by hand, pushing a lever back and forth which jostled the clothes. When she thought the clothes were washed enough, she drained the water. Next she put more hot water in the washer and pushed the handle back and forth to rinse the clothes.

When she thought she had done that enough, she stopped, picked the clothes out one at a time, rung the water out of them by hand, and then hung them on clotheslines in the backyard to dry. Grandma called Monday "wash day" for good reason.

The clothes washer was one old piece of technology used on that farm. My grandfather worked his 160 acres with four horses which pulled a variety of implements that plowed the earth, cultivated between the rows of plants, and even mowed his lawn. Neither grandparent complained about their lives. They understood what needed to be done to make a living and they did it. The changes between that agricultural environment of the 1940s and the world today is nothing like what is coming toward us in the twenty-first century. The sooner we get ready for what is on the horizon in the next five to thirty years, the better. We cannot be caught off guard or flat-footed. We must be prepared.

Chapter One

Disruption Tsunami(s)

In 2019, life is good. Things are normal in the country's community colleges and universities. Students enroll, take courses, attend sporting events, enjoy each other, graduate, and head out into the world of work or senior institutions of higher education. They use Facebook, Twitter, Instagram, email, and other communication technologies. Most likely they may have heard of autonomous cars, drones, 3-D printing, nanotechnology, Watson, Bitcoin/Blockchain, and personal robots.

They may have heard less about the Internet of Things, the human and agricultural genome development, artificial intelligence, and quantum computing. However, many of those who have heard about the many twenty-first-century technologies will probably file them in the category of science fiction or new things that might become reality in the far-off future. Certainly, nothing to worry about today.

How about the leaders and faculty of community colleges and universities? How aware are they of the multitude of digital technologies about to impinge on their worlds? If they are aware of some of them, how concerned are they about them? New technologies are being developed all the time, but they do not seem to have much of an effect on higher education. Email has become as normal as electric lights. Facebook is part and parcel of daily life. Even the president of the United States uses Twitter. Nothing much is changing. Or is it?

HIGHER ED IN THE TWENTY-FIRST CENTURY

The author of this book is a professor at Wingate University. One course he teaches is titled "The Community College in the Twenty-First Century." The focus of that course is to help graduate students working on their doctorate in higher education administration understand what will face them in their future leadership careers. When the course was first taught, one assignment for the students was to research what current leaders in higher education, business leaders, state legislators, congressmen, and students thought was coming that would affect higher education in the next five to twenty years.

The graduate students were diligent in their research and interviewed a wide variety of individuals who might have some ideas where things were going in the future for higher education. The upshot of the research showed that most interviewees did not think much past one year to a year and a half. Almost none were willing to guess about ten years out and only a rare individual had any ideas about 20 years or more. As things turned out, the assignment was of little help for the future careers of the students. It was necessary to look elsewhere to see what would be useful to them.

In further research for the course, the author read a number of books on the various technologies and came across the World Future Society, Artificial General Intelligence Society, Defense Advanced Research Projects Agency (DARPA), Federation of Robotics, dozens of other organizations, and future-focused authors, all trying to peer into the future. They wanted to understand how a variety of technologies would impact the business community, life in general, politics, and culture. However, very few made an effort to describe how the technologies might impact higher education in the future.

As a result, a new assignment was developed which asked the students to research one of ten technologies that were in the process of developing and would definitely exist in the next five to twenty years. All of them it turned out would have an effect on community colleges and universities, their missions, visions, and daily operations. Further, it became clear that those ten technologies were going to have considerable impacts on life in general, society, and culture.

The graduate students became very interested, researched thoroughly, and produced results that showed that due to technological change, serious paradigmatic leadership change was just around the corner. That finding was very eye-opening to the graduate students as they looked to the future of higher education.

INKLINGS OF THE FUTURE

Even though it may appear at the moment that no drastic changes are on the horizon, some recent consumer items provide insight into the front edge possibilities. Facebook, Instagram, and Twitter came on the scene and were quite easy to adapt to and use. Now one can keep up with family and friends with little effort. Many are already wondering how they ever lived without Amazon Echo. A few find Tesla's almost autonomous car a real wonder; it really works as advertised.

Most people probably assume that as new things come into existence there will be time to learn about them, try them out, and get used to them. After all, people adapted in the twentieth century to the telephone, electricity, automobiles, radio, TV, DVDs, CDs, and airplanes. Those technologies developed in a linear fashion, one day at a time, one year at a time, a decade at a time. There was plenty of time to become aware of them, understand them, and ultimately use them as they came along.

The assumption is that in the twenty-first century, technologies will develop in much the same way with plenty of time to incorporate new things into one's life. However, that assumption is incorrect. In the current century, technology no longer develops in a linear manner. It develops exponentially. Although the current iPhone X may seem like just another development in a long line of cell phones, from the bag phone in the 1990s to the computer phone in 2018, it did not just happen by chance, good luck, or in a linear fashion.

The development from bag phone to cell phone computer happened because of Moore's Law, which states that computer power will double every 18 months. In late 1950s, one transistor could be placed on a silicon chip. By the early 1970s, 2,300 transistors could be place on one chip. By 2018, thanks to the continuous doubling every 18 months, 30 billion transistors could be placed on one chip (Fingas, 2017). That doubling process, which most likely will remain active for many more years, now creates additional computer power and data storage developing at an exponential rate.

exponential development, not linear

HOCKEY STICK METAPHOR

An easy way to understand something developing exponentially is to visualize a hockey stick. It has two parts. The blade is basically flat with a slight rise toward the shaft. The shaft goes up almost vertically from the blade. The development of the transistor chip developed in an apparent linear fashion for a number of years, increasing gradually, one step at a time, along the blade of the hockey stick. However, by the time the year 2000 came along, the increase in power was stretching toward the shaft and by 2010, it was going up the shaft at a ferocious rate of speed.

STAGES OF EXPONENTIAL TECHNOLOGY

The growth of an exponential technology has two stages. First, for a period of time it develops on a linear scale and not much seems to be happening. Second, it reaches a point where the doubling process causes it to expand at an unanticipated, exponential velocity far beyond the linear progression. Technologies connected to the computer world, like the Internet for example, appear to be in the background with not much happening until that certain point is reached on the blade and then they take off up the shaft of hockey stick.

CHESSBOARD ANALOGY

Another way to help exponential development make sense is to consider the following analogy. Place a chessboard on the floor; it has 64 squares upon which pieces of the chess game could be played. Instead of chess pieces, try this doubling process. Place one penny on the first square at the bottom of the board, on the square next to it place two pennies, on the third square place four pennies, the fourth square eight pennies, the fifth square 16 pennies, the sixth square 32 pennies. Continue doubling the number of pennies square by square: seven gets 64, eight gets 128, nine 256, ten 512, eleven 1,024, twelve 2,048, or $20.48. By the time the 26th square is reached, the penny doubling number is 33,544,432 or $335,444.32. Penny doubling the amount square by square seems gradual for many squares, but by halfway through the chessboard, at the thirty-second square, the number increases to approximately $20.8 million. Quite a pile of pennies.

If the penny doubling continued to square number 64, the number of pennies is probably more than all the money in the world put together. The penny-doubling analogy demonstrates what happens in an exponential process. This process must be understood in order to explain what happens with an exponentially developing technology. It moves along slowly for a period of time and then takes off like a rocket at a certain point.

EXPONENTIAL TECHNOLOGIES

The technologies listed at the beginning of this chapter all operate in an exponential manner, mostly because all of them use computer power that is directly affected by Moore's Law, power doubling every 18 months. Along with that, computer storage develops at the same rate.

In other words, the technologies do not develop like the telephone, electricity, gasoline engines, televisions, cars, or airplanes did in the twentieth century. Artificial intelligence, autonomous vehicles, Bitcoin/Blockchain, 3-D printing, genome development, the Internet of Things, nanotechnology, personal robots, and quantum computing all develop in an exponential manner.

SERIAL DISRUPTIVE TSUNAMIS

That kind of increase can make the technologies appear like an unexpected tsunami. In a most disruptive manner, each technology will cause change on its own, which is disconcerting enough. However, when they appear one after the other, they arrive like serial disruptive tsunamis. As they follow each other, each technology will bring serious change, allowing very little time to adjust or adapt to them.

If there was only one technology in the exponential future, it might be dealt with in a reasonable manner. However, when there are multiple technologies, the era of serial disruptions becomes a reality. It will make reacting to them in reasonable, linear manner most difficult, if not almost impossible (Hyacinth, 2017).

IMPACT ON HIGHER EDUCATION

Community colleges and universities will be directly affected. Higher education leaders and faculty must be prepared. The turnaround time will be short. Trying to catch up after the disruptions will be most difficult. To be unaware and unprepared will potentially lead to disaster. Learning to unlearn past behavior and relearn successful future behavior will be critical to all concerned in order for community colleges and universities to remain viable, useful, and successful.

It will not be long before an individual will get into an autonomous car, direct it through the GPS system to take one to the medical clinic where the doctor will modify the genome to address the illness the person has been experiencing, and insert sensors into the body. The sensors will transmit data of bodily functions to the cloud, which will be read by algorithms and reviewed by the doctor to see how the patient is progressing.

Science fiction? Maybe today, but with already existing technologies, very soon it will be science fact, a reality that everyone will have to learn to live with. What does this mean for the community college and the university? In general, higher education will be in the middle of things. As examples, the university will create the sensors and the algorithms; the community college will produce the workforce needed in the health and the transportation fields. Jobs that never existed before will suddenly be needed, posthaste. Training for them will be critical.

If institutions of higher education are not properly prepared, they will be hard pressed to deal with the impact of the technologies. On the other hand, community colleges and universities which are prepared will be able to take action for the good of all concerned. It is critical to the survival of institutions of higher education to be prepared if they wish to remain viable and successful in the digital world.

PREPARING FOR THE FUTURE

- Although educational leaders may have heard of the ten technologies developing in the early twenty-first century, as they go their daily routines, everything seems normal.

- In the "Community College in the Twenty-First Century" course, part of the EdD program for community college leaders at Wingate University, research for future trends began with interviewing leaders in higher education, business, and politics where it was found that almost none thought further ahead than one and a half years.
- The course changed to researching the development of ten technologies and how and when they would impact higher education.
- It appears that most people make an assumption that the ten technologies will develop in the twenty-first century at the same pace as others had done in the twentieth.
- In the twenty-first century, technology no longer develops in a linear manner as it had in the twentieth century.
- In the twenty-first century technology develops in an exponential manner.
- The hockey stick metaphor and the chessboard analogy help one to understand how the exponential speed of technology works. It is very different from the linear manner.
- The ten technologies discussed in this book most likely will appear in a serial manner, one after the other, or in some cases simultaneously.
- Exponential technologies coming on the scene sequentially or simultaneously allow very little time for adjustment and adaptation to them.
- Community college and university leaders must be prepared to deal with the disruptions that will be created as the technologies reach rapid acceleration.
- Institutions of higher education that are properly prepared will have a chance at working successfully with the impact of the technologies. Those who are not prepared will find them most difficult to deal with.

Chapter Two

Digital Technologies

Near Term

In the early twenty-first century, as the leaders in community colleges and universities woke up in the morning and headed off to another day of work, they tended to see things happening in a linear fashion, one day at a time, one week at a time, one month at a time, and one year at a time. Their worlds were moving ahead in a reasonable, predictable manner. The big concerns on the leaders' minds might be how much funding was coming from the legislature, was retention working favorably, or were there were any issues with the fund-raising project?

In their busy day-to-day existence, they may have been unaware that a number of technologies were developing on an exponential track, offstage from their working environments. If the administrators had heard of the technologies, they may have decided to be concerned about them later. What they were not taking into account was that each technology holds the potential to disrupt not only the lives and work of educational leaders, but also the institution, the students, their communities, and society itself (Ford, 2015).

SERIAL DISRUPTION

There are ten technologies currently developing in the exponential realm, which will directly affect community colleges and universities. They are 3-D printing, autonomous vehicles, the Internet of Things, genome: medical, genome: agricultural, personal robots, Bitcoin/Blockchain, artificial intelligence, nanotechnology, and quantum computing.

These must be monitored continually as to determine when they might suddenly appear as if from nowhere. As these technologies begin to become disruptive realities, each will have an impact on community colleges and universities. "We have to recognize that every job will be enabled or disrupted by technology. It is just a matter of when, what, and how technology gets applied to the job" (Meister, 2017, p. 217). Further, as the technologies intermingle and overlap with each other, they have the potential of creating an era of serial disruptions.

Leaders and faculty in community colleges and universities cannot be caught flat-footed. They must be on the lookout for the rapid expansion of the technologies that will directly impact their institution, administrators, faculty, staff, students, programs, equipment, facilities, and the communities and/or states they serve. Educational leaders must become aware of the disruptions the technologies will create and learn how to prepare for and deal with them when they arrive.

3-D PRINTING (ADDITIVE MANUFACTURING)

3-D Printing, also known as Additive Manufacturing, is one of the ten technologies that is already included in many community colleges and universities. 3-D printing has the potential to make serious changes in the construction and manufacturing industries. It also will appear in the health organizations.

To understand the impact 3-D printing could have in the near future, one only needs to look back at the 1980s when the personal computer first came on the scene. Initially, the PC was just a toy; recall the Commodore computer, for instance. But within five to ten years, the personal computer was not only found on the desks of the clerical assistants but also on the desks of staff, faculty, and administrators.

By the 1990s, the personal computer made its way into households with programs not just made for work, but also for play, social interaction, and home efficiency. As computer power expanded exponentially, the PC became less expensive and more pervasive. Most everyone thought they needed one and a large percentage of the population in developed countries obtained one. In a little more than two additional decades, the power of the personal computer was transferred to the cell phone. By 2018, the iPhone X and other cell phones were actually computers with a phone, which almost everyone carried.

3-D printing has the potential to be on a similar track. It already is home-bound to some extent. It already can create accurate products in plastic, metal, concrete, and wood. The product to be created can be scanned and inputted or inserted by means of a design from a computer. There seems to be no end in sight as to what it can produce. It will soon be useful not only in the workplace, but in the home as well.

The question is how long will 3-D printing take to become a staple in every household? Will it take as long as the PC or will it develop and expand faster? Whatever the speed of becoming commonplace in the home, it will arrive. Consumers will find it useful. It will have an impact on everyday living and working.

Today, the layering system of 3-D printing takes some time to produce a product, but in the near future that time will be reduced very significantly. Compare a 1985 PC to a 2018 PC, in terms of software, size, capabilities, and extent of use. It is easy to visualize a 3-D printer developing on a similar path (Barnatt, 2016).

3-D PRINTING: HUMAN HEALTH

Not only is 3-D printing useful for manufacturing things out of steel, wood, and plastic, but it is also able to produce organs of the human body, such as a liver or lung. Since human organs are specific to the human being involved, mass production of body parts is not a useful venture. A viable process to develop body organs from scratch for specific individual humans had not been known to exist until 3-D printing arrived on the scene. It has the potential to expand exponentially in the medical world.

Although the possibility of making a human organ using 3-D printing may seem like science fiction, in fact, there is considerable research under way to construct body parts for use in the very near future. The creation of new body parts that are inserted in the human body as replacements for the original defective or diseased organ has the potential to become the norm within a decade.

3-D printing will have an impact on the mission and vision of the community college and the university, and it is already becoming an instructional tool in classrooms and labs in high schools. Students will soon be enrolling at the community college and university with experience with 3-D printing at the high school level. They will expect to receive further instruction at the higher education institution. 3-D printing arena for training and education could create a change in the mission and vision of the college and university (Friedman, 2016).

AUTONOMOUS VEHICLES

The autonomous vehicle is another technology that is approaching the up-tick of the hockey stick metaphor. Companies like Tesla, Google, Apple, General Motors, Ford, Volvo, BMW, VW, and others are already moving ahead with the design and development of what in the very near future will become totally autonomous cars and trucks.

As an automotive example, the Tesla Model S already has the technology for self-driving on the interstate. The driver can push a button, remove hands from the wheel, and allow the car to drive itself at a preset cruise control speed. When the car approaches another vehicle going slower, the Tesla will slow down. If the vehicle in front comes to a complete stop, so will the Tesla. Hands off.

When the car reaches home, the driver can leave the car outside of the garage and push a button. The car will open the garage door, drive itself into the garage, close the garage door, shut itself off, and electronically connect to the battery charger, a plate on the floor under the car. The Tesla is not a totally autonomous vehicle at present, but it is rapidly developing in that direction.

TIMING FOR AUTONOMOUS VEHICLES

Many questions about autonomous cars and trucks need to be answered. Will there be consumer interest in purchasing an autonomous car? When will regulations developed by the state and federal governments be completed to allow them on road nationwide? Will roadside signage be changed to an electronically readable format? As an example of how fast the movement toward autonomous cars is progressing, Uber recently agreed to purchase 24,000 autonomous cars from Volvo (West, 2018).

None of these questions are impossible to answer, but they will take some time to resolve. Meanwhile, expect to see additional computer products placed into the automobile that will make it more reasonable and safe to drive. The National Highway Traffic Safety Administration (NHTSA), a division of the U.S. Department of Transportation, outlined the five levels of autonomous vehicles.

Level 0—No Automation: The full-time performance by the human driver of all aspects of the dynamic driving task, even when enhanced by warning or intervention systems

Level 1—Driver Assistance: The driving mode-specific execution by a driver assistance system of either steering or acceleration/deceleration using information about the driving environment and with the expectation that the human driver performs all remaining aspects of the dynamic driving task

Level 2—Partial Automation: The driving mode-specific execution by one or more driver assistance systems of both steering and acceleration/ deceleration using information about the driving environment and with the expectation that the human driver performs all remaining aspects of the dynamic driving task

Level 3—Conditional Automation: The driving mode-specific performance by an Automated Driving System of all aspects of the dynamic driving task with the expectation that the human driver will respond appropriately to a request to intervene

Level 4—High Automation: The driving mode-specific performance by an Automated Driving System of all aspects of the dynamic driving task, even if a human driver does not respond appropriately to a request to intervene

Level 5—Full Automation: The full-time performance by an Automated Driving System of all aspects of the dynamic driving task under all roadway and environmental conditions that can be managed by a human driver (Hyatt, et al., 2018, pp. 5–8)

AUTONOMOUS TRUCKS

The question of the success of the autonomous automobile is one thing. The other is the autonomous truck. Tesla already has a prototype; Google has

Waymo (Hawkins, 2018). Self-driving trucks are now delivering refrigerators from El Paso, Texas, to Palm Springs, California (Davies, 2017). The impact on the current trucking industry could be dramatic. Currently, approximately three million individuals in the United States drive trucks for a living. A high percentage of them could be replaced by autonomous trucks.

 When autonomous trucks become a reality, what will the displaced truckers do? This is where the community college must be prepared. Retraining of truckers to learn new skills in the digital age could be a daunting task. Although there will be many new jobs developed to support the technologies impacting business and industry, most will require skills in math, computers, and science. These areas of study may be foreign to many truck drivers.

DISPLACED TRUCKERS AND COMMUNITY COLLEGES

Community colleges can expect to see a significant increase in their developmental studies programs to bring the displaced workers up to the educational levels needed for success in the job world of technologies. In addition, many other low-skill jobs will be replaced with digital formats. The individuals who are displaced will head back to community colleges to learn the skills for the new jobs. Developmental studies will be critical for many of them and community colleges will need to be prepared.

THE INTERNET OF THINGS

The Internet of Things (IoT) already exists to some extent, but the development of the technology is still on the metaphorical blade of the hockey stick closing in on the shaft. The IoT will soon find itself integrated into existing businesses that are interested in discovering what the data reveals about the operation, quality, and life span of their products (Schwab, 2016).

The development of the IoT is happening with limited public notice or concern. Consumers are already buying goods and products that have RFID sensors inserted into them. They are about the size of a grain of rice, almost unobservable in the products into which they are connected. Further, they are inexpensive to add to a product, and most important, they send data to the cloud for storage. Data storage has dropped in cost to pennies per gigabyte of storage, which makes storing data inexpensive.

Since the IoT is already functional to a considerable degree, data on a wide variety of things are being collected and stored. National research organizations forecast that by 2020 somewhere between 26 billion to 212 billion sensors will be transmitting information to the Internet and on to the cloud (Miller, 2015). By 2025, the number of sensors sending information to the cloud is expected to reach one trillion (Schwab, 2016). Whatever the actual number, there will be a huge amount of stored information that can be accessed, analyzed, and used. Who will use all this collected and stored information?

Users of the IoT

Manufacturers

First, the manufacturer who produced the item will want to know where its products were bought, how long they lasted, what kind of unforeseen problems were created, how many units are still in inventory, and how many more items should be manufactured. That kind of information will be a boon to the manufacturer that is interested in continuous improvement and sale of its products.

Retailers

The second group interested in the data are the retailers who will want to know how many items sold, how fast, what kinds of problems were involved with the product, and how many need to be ordered for future consumption. Data analysis will create the transparency of the quality, function, and life span of manufactured products.

Consumers

Third, the consumer will have access to some of the information garnered. If something is about to go wrong with a smart refrigerator, television, computer, automobile, and other smart products, the unit will inform the owner, most likely through a screen built into it. As a result, the consumer will become aware of problems with the item before they occur and can react in a timely manner.

Sensors

Fourth, the sensors will communicate with each other using the Internet. For example, autonomous cars on the highway will be able to communicate with each other and travel together in packs, much closer together than normal highway driving, which could allow for more rapid movement from point to point. Smart devices in the home, such as the refrigerator, could be easily programmed by the owner to contact the repair man directly and schedule a time for a maintenance visit. Of course, that would be done using the owner's calendar, also found on the Internet (Miller, 2015).

Managers

Fifth, managers in many different organizations will access the cloud concerning products directly and/or will hire data analysts to review the information received. With the data in hand, the managers will determine how to deal with and react to the information created by the sensors in their products that are sending information to the cloud. New jobs will develop, some similar to those that exist at present and others that do not currently exist due to the amount and types of information that will be available.

Entrepreneurial Opportunities

Sixth, beyond existing businesses, new entrepreneurial businesses may develop, which will need a workforce that does not exist in 2019. The community college will need to react rapidly to serve the local workforce needs. The university will need to get involved with the development of the algorithm needs of the businesses. By 2025, one trillion sensors are expected to be connected to the Internet from everything from automobiles to home appliances to the home itself (Schwab, 2016).

New Jobs

Finally, there will be jobs not currently imagined. Certainly data analysts will be needed by business and government. Cybersecurity will become critical, which will significantly increase the workforce in that area. Further, there may be many uses for the information that have not come to light at the present. The IoT could become a workforce bonanza, which will have a positive impact on community colleges and universities (Miller, 2015).

A survey of 800 business executives conducted by the World Economic Forum in 2015 found that 89 percent of the respondents expected a tipping point to occur in the field of the Internet of Things by 2025 (Schwab, 2016). This tipping point could lead to investors and entrepreneurs envisioning new businesses to deal with the phenomenal amount of data that will be stored in the cloud. Opportunities will exist; jobs will be created. The community colleges and universities must be prepared to create new programs, certifications, and short courses.

ENTREPRENEURIAL EDUCATION

Further, the community college and the university will be impacted by the need for programs of study focused on entrepreneurial education. There may be a considerable number of totally new businesses engendered by the IoT. Since the concept is so new and not fully understood, the IoT will require inventive minds to figure out the most successful ways to create education and training for the kinds of jobs the data-collecting mammoth will require.

> Amid all the possibilities, one fact stands out: the Internet of Things will revolutionize both developing and developed nations and introduce a tidal wave of commercial and consumer applications—from smarter utility grids and smart cars to radically different health care and manufacturing systems. It will change our perspective of the world and usher in automation and entirely new ways of interacting with the world around us. (Greengard, 2015, p. 172.)

GENOME: MEDICAL

Genome development in the medical and agricultural fields is developing rapidly along the blade of the metaphorical hockey stick. They could move to the shaft of the stick in the very near future. At the moment, this field is developing mostly in the shadows rather than out front. In 2003, the Human Genome Project spent $2.7 billion to create the first entire genome. By 2009, the cost had dropped to $100K. In 2018, the cost to sequence a human genome was less than $100.

The reductions in cost are due to the increase of computer power generated according to Moore's law. The impact on human beings and agriculture is phenomenal. Thanks to a process titled Clustered Regularity Interspaced Short Palindromic Repeats (CRISPR) combined with an protein known as Cas9, CRISPR/Cas9, certain diseases will be cured. Parents will at some point in the near future be able to design the DNA of their children, and new food processes will be created (Doudna, 2017).

The possibilities will exist and most likely will be used by those in the medical field on a regular basis. Even if the United States passed a law against human DNA engineering, other countries would move ahead using the potential of that possibility. The potential for generations of brilliant, extremely healthy, long-lived human beings will be too much to ignore. On the negative side, it could lead to a military made up of cyber-humans with powers far beyond current humans, a rather frightening possibility.

GENOME: AGRICULTURE

In addition, genome development has entered the agricultural world. Today an animal's genome can be changed. A pig can be made more muscular with less fat with the change in the genome rather than a lengthy process of breeding. The same can be done for food. The genome of corn might be changed to increase the yield on the cob or change the color, if that were of interest. The possibilities are endless and can take place in a very short period of time.

The genome future will affect both community colleges and universities. Community colleges will develop additional associate degree and certificate programs for students entering the medical fields. At the university level, research into possibilities of disease control, the aging process, and others may create entirely new career paths to pursue. New programs and disciplines will appear to support them at the community college and university levels.

PERSONAL ROBOTS

Although manufacturing robots have been around for decades and have made significant inroads and successes in the construction of automobiles and other mechanical devices, what is in the immediate future is different. Personal robots are first being seen in such items as Alexa, Echo, Siri, and other electronic devices. These devices can play music, answer questions, solve basic math problems, read a story, control lighting, and adjust air-conditioning. They are the leading edge of what is to come.

Japanese companies have been developing personal robots that look and talk like human beings that can give directions, serve food, and provide elementary support to human beings. Japan began developing personal robots to serve its elderly population. The diet in Japan is extremely healthy and as a result, the Japanese tend to live longer.

Since the country is made up of a set of mountainous islands and suitable living space is limited, bringing in immigrants to provide services to the elderly is not possible. As a result, the Japanese decided on an alternative strategy, that of developing personal robots to provide the services the aging population will need.

The Japanese have been working on the development of personal robots since 2005; they have made considerable headway. The Honda Corporation developed a robot that can walk and talk called ASIMO. Although this robot is able to perform many basic functions that an elderly person would need, the Japanese have moved ahead into developing personal robots that look like human beings. They are already a long way down the path to making personal robots that appear human a reality (Ford, 2015).

Other countries such as South Korea, China, England, France, and Germany have jumped into the development of personal robots as well. If there is any doubt as to whether these robots actually exist, one only needs to check the Internet to find examples. Even the United States has done considerable work in the area. The personal robot originally called Baxter, now known as Sawyer, can perform a great number of functions and is easy to program (Ford, 2015). It is available at a reasonable cost, some $25,000. If it is well-received, expect the price to drop considerably.

Community colleges and universities will soon find this technology at their respective doorsteps. Personal robots will need maintenance and repair, which will lead to training programs at the community college. The university will be involved in the design of personal robots with the internal computers that will need development in terms of hardware and software. Further, job opportunities, not even on the drawing board at present, will be needed to support this exponentially developing technology.

BITCOIN/BLOCKCHAIN

Bitcoin/Blockchain is an alternative, digital financial system. The idea of a digital financial system dates back to 1993 when David Chaum, a mathematician, developed eCash. Unfortunately, Chaum's company went bankrupt in 1998 (Tapscott and Tapscott, 2016). Bitcoin/Blockchain appeared in 2008 supposedly as the result of the Great Recession. It came from a Japanese source, Satoshi Nakamoto, a single person or a group, whose identity has been kept secret (Tapscott and Tapscott, 2016).

Bitcoin is a form of money which can be purchased with dollars, euros, yens, rubles, or any other monetary source. The Bitcoin/Blockchain system has since been used by individuals, most legally, some questionably, to transmit funds through the system. The integrity of the system is ensured through heavy-duty encryption known as cryptography. There is no bank or country involved in the transactions.

> Bitcoin or other digital currency isn't saved in a file somewhere; it's represented by transactions recorded in a blockchain—kind of like a global spreadsheet or ledger, which leverages the resources of a large peer-to-peer bitcoin network to verify and approve each bitcoin transaction. Each blockchain, like the one that uses bitcoin, is *distributed*: it runs on computers provided by volunteers around the world; there is no central database to hack. (Tapscott and Tapscott, 2016, p. 6)

A Bitcoin exists in a block in the cloud and can only be spent by its owner. When an owner spends a portion of the Bitcoin, the transaction creates a new block which is connected to the original block from which the funding was removed. As more portions of the Bitcoin is spent, each a transaction creates a block that is connected to the previous block, creating a Blockchain. This entire process is transparent to the owner.

Bitcoin transactions are secured by cryptography that supposedly cannot be hacked; however, individuals have found that the transaction can be hacked during the second(s) of the actual transaction. In 2010 such a hack took place with the hacker absconding with hefty financial gains (Gates, 2017). That problem has been rectified, but no one knows when the next successful hack may occur.

This financial system is developing but as yet has not become foolproof. However, considerable effort will be made during the next decade to improve the processes and make the entire system non-hackable, those interested in the system believe.

If the Bitcoin/Blockchain system can be made secure for all transactions, then this technology will affect community colleges and universities in the future. There will be opportunities for short courses, certificates, and most likely entire degrees. Perhaps future students will want to pay tuition and fees with Bitcoin. This is a technology to watch, not ignore.

CONCLUSION

A number of technologies are developing in the twenty-first century that will have a direct impact on community colleges and universities. Each of them are developing in an exponential manner, which means they may be well known because they are already in the open, or they may be relatively unknown because they are developing offstage. They all will become noticeable when they reach the ultra-rapid exponential stage. Leaders in higher education need to be aware of them, ready to deal with them, or suffer the disruptions they will create.

PREPARING FOR THE FUTURE

- Community college and university leaders most likely assume that leading an institution in the twenty-first century will be very similar to that in the twentieth.
- Living in a linear world is relatively reasonable.
- Technologies are developing offstage from normal life and are easy to ignore.
- There are 10 technologies currently developing that will directly affect higher education.

- The 10 technologies must be monitored for their development continually so that leaders in higher education are not caught flat-footed.
- 3-D printing has a tremendous potential for changing construction, manufacturing, and health industries.
- 3-D printing may follow a pathway similar to that of the PC in the 1980s.
- A variety of products can be made from plastic, metal, concrete, and wood using 3-D printing.
- As the layering process shortens in the 3-D printing process, the importance of this technology will increase tremendously.
- 3-D printing will soon be used in the health industry to produce organs for the human body.
- Students enrolling in community colleges and universities in the near future will most likely have experience with 3-D printing from their high school education.
- Autonomous vehicles are rapidly being developed on both the automobile and truck levels.
- Tesla, Google, Apple, General Motors, Ford, Volvo, BMW, and VW are developing the technology for autonomous vehicles.
- A considerable number of questions will need to be answered before autonomous cars and trucks will become commonplace on American highways.
- The National Highway Traffic Safety Administration has outlined five levels of autonomous vehicles.
- When autonomous trucks become normal in the transportation of goods, the number of displaced truck drivers will be significant.
- Community colleges will serve the displaced truckers with training and education.
- Finding appropriate jobs for displaced truckers may be difficult.
- The Internet of Things is developing with very little public notice or interest.
- RFID sensors will have significant impact on manufactured products.
- The IoT could produce a workforce bonanza.
- By 2025, one trillion sensors will be sending information to the cloud.
- The users of the IoT will include manufacturers, retailers, consumers, managers, new entrepreneurial businesses, and jobs not currently in existence.

- The IoT will produce the need for entrepreneurial education at the community college and university levels.
- The IoT may produce a number of new businesses.
- Genome development in the medical field has phenomenal opportunities for curing diseases to allowing parents to design the DNA of their children.
- CRISPR/Cas9, which allows for easy revision of the genome structure, has potential for positive and negative uses.
- Genome development in the agricultural world makes it easy to modify food products in a very short period of time.
- Personal robots are being developed rapidly, especially in Japan where robots are being produced that look and act like human beings.
- Japanese personal robots will serve the aging population of the country.
- The Japanese have made tremendous headway with robot development since 2005.
- Community colleges will find training and education needs for the repair and maintenance of personal robots.
- Many other countries are working on the development of personal robots as well.
- Bitcoin and Blockchain form an alternative financial system that exists but at the moment has possible security issues. However, most likely those will be corrected in the near future.
- Bitcoin has been used by individuals since 2008.
- Bitcoin exists in the cloud only accessible by its owner.
- The Bitcoin/Blockchain technology could affect community colleges and universities in the future with new program offerings.

Chapter Three

Digital Technologies

The Big Three

Looking toward the future in terms of technologies, there are three big elephants in the room. One technology develops using Moore's law; the other two develop in the quantum world. All three technologies are extreme game-changers for human life and work. All three are presently on the blade of the metaphorical hockey, but when any one of the three, let alone all three at once or in succession, hits the shaft, all predictions as to what may result are guesses or estimates at best. The three big elephants in the room are artificial general intelligence, nanotechnology, and quantum computing.

ARTIFICIAL INTELLIGENCE (AI)

Artificial intelligence (AI) in the foreseeable future will most likely use silicon chips in its development. Moore's law, in existence since 1965, states that the number of transistors on a chip doubles every 18 months. That doubling process has led to the fact that 30 billion transistors exist on a chip in 2018. So far, only something called narrow AI—specific, limited AI—has been developed successfully as a result of that doubling process.

DEEP BLUE

Narrow AI allowed for the development of Deep Blue, an IBM computer that won a series of matches against the legendary chess player Garry Kasparov (Kasparov, 2017). The win did not happen on the first try by

Deep Blue; it took a few years of enhancement, but it was successful in 1997. Deep Blue is an example of narrow AI in that it is limited to playing chess. Interestingly, that computer was no longer used after 1997.

WATSON

Some years later IBM developed another narrow AI computer called Watson, which took on the two best *Jeopardy* players, Ken Jennings and Brad Rutter, and beat them both in 2011 (Baker, 2011). The wins by Deep Blue and Watson hark back to races between horses and early steam locomotives. The new technology took the flag every time. Does that mean that Watson or Deep Blue are suddenly going to take over the world?

The answer for is no. There is a reason for that. Both of these computers, as originally configured, could accomplish only one thing, win over a human being at chess or win against human beings at *Jeopardy*. Neither Watson nor Deep Blue could do more than their program allowed; both were limited or narrow in their abilities.

WATSON REPROGRAMMED

However, over the past years, the Watson computer has been reprogrammed in other narrow AI capacities. A Watson computer was reprogrammed to accumulate all the data pertaining to the disease of cancer and the procedures to deal with it. Watson's purpose was to assist oncologists more rapidly come to conclusions as to the best procedures to serve an individual cancer patient. Although the ability of the computer is significant and important to those dealing with the disease, its power still lies in the category of narrow AI.

THE SINGULARITY

Futurist Ray Kurzweil forecasts that, given Moore's law, the power in a computer will be advanced to the point where it will have the ability to match the mind of a human being, something called a Singularity. "I set the date for the Singularity—representing a profound and disruptive transformation in human capacity—as 2045" (Kurzweil, 2006, p. 136). At that point in time, the computer will have reached what Kurzweil calls artificial general intelligence (AGI). This computer could have an estimated IQ of perhaps 600.

ARTIFICIAL GENERAL INTELLIGENCE

Artificial general intelligence (AGI) is very different from narrow AI. An AGI computer will literally be able to think like a human being. It could play chess and Jeopardy, analyze problems facing the human race, develop scenarios for solving them, and, with a minimal amount of effort, cause changes in the digital world without human programming. That makes an AGI computer very powerful with abilities that could affect human beings both positively and negatively. Further, it could create its own programming.

Interestingly, the medical version of the Watson computer did not have a person or group input all the information about cancer patients, procedures, results, and the like; rather it was programmed to input the information directly from digital sources. In that kind of programming, the computer could soon learn all the information ever reported digitally about the disease, patients, procedures, medications, and so forth. In other words, it moved ahead a little bit into the world of a non-narrow AI. Although the thought of a narrow AI getting wider is interesting, there is another situation to be considered.

ARTIFICIAL SUPER INTELLIGENCE

If the doubling process predicted by Moore's law continues after the artificial general intelligence is reached, within two to five years of further doubling the computer will have reached what Kurzweil calls artificial super intelligence (ASI). This computer could have an estimated IQ of a million or more. Such an ASI computer could probably figure out how to keep the exponential rise of computer power going far into the future.

If that were to happen, the forecasters envision the possibility that the computer would be so far beyond the human mind that the world as we know it could be changed phenomenally. Worst case scenario, the forecast of an ASI computer has led to the prediction of the extinction of the human race as computers might take over the world and find humans worthless (Barrat, 2013). That is a very serious consequence that must be considered, but there are other more positive possibilities as well.

CYBER-HUMANS

Some futurists envision the cyber-human, a human being with various computer chips being inserted into the human mind and body, making a person competitive with the ASI computer (Barfield, 2015). Of course, since computers are programmed by human beings, perhaps the computer could be programmed to never do anything that would create harm or danger to the human race.

On the other side of that coin is machine learning, which means that a programmed computer can be allowed to learn on its own. The medical version of Watson already has that capability in a limited field of inquiry. Where an Artificial Super Intelligence with the capacity to learn on its own might lead is something to think about.

LIFE IN THE TWENTIETH CENTURY

John Jones was five years old in 1918. He most likely heard about the war to end all wars, but did not really understand it. A relative of his did die unexpectedly of the 1919 world flu epidemic, but since his immediate family was not affected, that probably did not mean too much to him. He graduated from eighth grade and went to work in a gas station during the Great Depression. Later he completed an apprenticeship in the tin smith trade.

Fast forward to 1950: he was married for eleven years, had three children, had his own house built, and was working as an electrician in the housing boom following World War II. Although things had changed a lot in this life, he had a car, house, washing machine, refrigerator, radio, phonograph, and lots of things that did not exist in his childhood. Overall, he thought the changes were all for the good and he and his family were living a decent life. He had been able to keep up with all the new things that came his way. He passed away in 2000.

LIFE IN THE TWENTY-FIRST CENTURY

John's grandson Randy was born in 2001. He had his first computer when he was four years old, a castoff from his parents. By the time he reached high school his was using his third computer, which his parents had bought specifically for him. As a senior in high school he had an iPhone, Apple Watch, loads of video games, and his own car. Life looks good him. He has kept up with the technological changes and thinks they are normal. By 2050, he will be 49. What will his life be like then?

John Jones experienced changes coming at him in a linear manner. His grandson will experience changes coming into his world exponentially. What will his grandson face? What will his family have to deal with? The technologies he will experience will be much different than those experienced by his grandfather. Exactly how his life will unfold will be interesting to watch. My sense is that he will adapt. Time will tell.

The comparison is fascinating on one hand and downright scary on the other. In three generations there was a move from early cars, trains, street cars, and no air-conditioning in homes to comforts in all facilities, various types of transportation, computers, and new everyday objects that are taken for granted. What about 2050 with the possibilities of ASI? Something to think about.

NANOTECHNOLOGY

The second big elephant in the room is nanotechnology, the process that could manufacture objects starting at the level of atoms.

Albert Einstein, as part of his doctoral dissertation, calculated the size of a single sugar molecule from experimental data on the diffusion of sugar in water. His work showed that each molecule measures about a nanometer in diameter. At the billionth of a meter, a nanometer is the essence of small. (*Scientific American*, 2002, p. 60)

The scientific study of what exists on the nano level needed a name to describe it. In 1974, Japanese engineer Norio Taniguchi combined "nano" with "technology" and coined the term "nanotechnology." The term was introduced in the United States by Eric Drexler in 1987 in his book, *Engines of Creation*. According to Drexler (1987), "What digital technologies did for information, sound, and images, atomically precise manufacturing (APM) can do for physical products" (p. 7).

Drexler (1987) sees in the APM system a kind of printer that uses atoms to build objects almost like the 3-D printing process. At the nanotechnology level, manufacturing could be done at the level of atoms. Supposedly an object could be designed and constructed at the atomic level, which would have the potential build almost anything imaginable, large or small.

Development Process

Although nanotechnology has been around since the late 1980s, up to this point in time it has continued very much on the metaphorical blade of the hockey stick. The reason for its slower development is that nanotechnology works with atoms and molecules. When a scientist works at that level, he or she is working in the quantum world where Newton's laws, which satisfactorily explain almost everything observed with the five senses in the daily world experienced by humans, do not exist. That is correct—they do not exist.

Further, scientists have found that atoms seem to have a mind of their own; they can easily go through the skin and body of a human being. They can only be worked with in extremely cold conditions. Given those difficult situations, progress has moved more slowly.

As scientists gradually become more successful with their work in the nano world, the possibilities for constructing things at the atomic level that could impact various kinds of construction are in the offing. In addition, if scientists can successfully learn to work at the atomic level, it is possible in the future that significant changes could be made to our world, our solar system, and perhaps the universe itself (Drexler, 1987).

Future Possibilities

The possibilities at the university and community college levels are phenomenal. However, the world in which nanotechnology is useful will be one far beyond anything that we comprehend today. Most likely it would create a world that 50 to 100 years from now will be totally unrecognizable to us. That will not stop entrepreneurs, inventive minds, and creative scientists and engineers from developing a nanotechnology world.

QUANTUM COMPUTING

The third big elephant in the room is quantum computing, which also operates in the quantum world. When successfully completed, a quantum computer will be phenomenally fast. It will make Moore's law look as if it were describing something going in reverse. A quantum computer does not use bits as in the silicon chip world, but qubits. A qubit uses a pair of atoms to provide pairs of ones and zeros, which increase the computing speed phenomenally. When sets of qubits work together, the speed only increases.

Differences in the Quantum World

The fact that atoms exist in two places at once, either in near proximity or far distant, is on one hand, a quandary that seems impossible to understand and, on the other, creates tremendous opportunities (Kisak, 2016). The quandary is for human beings who assume that everything in the observable world and universe operates according to Newton's laws. Nothing in the observable world and universe exists in two places at once. However, in the quantum world atoms have been proven do just that. It took Albert Einstein decades to finally accept that fact. He did not prove it to be true; other scientists did prove it in the mid twentieth century.

The quantum computer uses atoms, which have negatives and positives, becoming its ones and zeros, but since the atom exists in two places at once, it means the atom has two ones and two zeros. That dual location is called superposition (Kisak, 2016). To describe that phenomenon, scientists created a new word, *qubits*, to describe the basic level of quantum computer operation. That difference, without getting far into physics to explain how it works, allows the quantum computer, using qubits rather than bits, to increase the speed of its operation unimaginably.

That ability for an atom to be in two locations simultaneously can be harnessed to process information exponentially faster than the bits in a classical computer. It would appear that Moore's law needs to be replaced by a new term, something like Quantum Law.

Development of the Quantum Computer

Since 2001, universities in the United States, Canada, the United Kingdom, China, and other countries have been working on developing a quantum computer, with breakthroughs annually (Kisak, 2016). As a result of that work, "In December 2015 NASA publicly displayed the world's first fully operational $15 million quantum computer made by the Canadian company, D-Wave, at the Quantum Artificial Intelligence Laboratory at its Ames Research Center in California's Moffett Field" (Kisak, 2016, p. 7).

A country extremely serious about developing quantum computing is China. In Hefei, Anhui Province, in China, a $10 billion, 4,000,000 SF facility is being constructed to house a research center for quantum applications. This facility is slated to open in 2020 with two goals: researching quantum metrology and the development of a quantum computer (Lin and Singer, 2017). Competition in the development of quantum computing between East and West appears to be on the horizon.

In the world of quantum computing it is literally impossible to ascertain what higher education might look like, or if it would even be needed. While the Chinese are investing $10 billion in a four million square–foot facility used totally for the development of quantum metrology in quantum computing, the United States has universities and Defense Advanced Research Projects Agency (DARPA) working on quantum computing. It goes without saying that coming in first in the race to develop quantum computing is critical.

Impact on Higher Education

Once the community colleges or universities begin to get fully involved with the technologies discussed up to this point and with more to come, the mission and vision of the institutions will need to exponentially develop to keep up with them. Keeping up, it will be discovered, is not a one-step process. It is continual, a rapid, moving process.

It will require a growth mind-set on the part of leaders and faculty in higher education. The new status quo will be continual, rapid change.

Business as usual will become business continually developing at a rapid pace. Further, it will mean at the community college and university that programs and courses will need to be continually revised to keep up with the technology, and of course, continual research to determine what is on the bleeding edge and how soon it will affect the institutions.

Redefined Business as Usual

As the result of the impacts of a number of technologies on community colleges and universities, the concept of business as usual will be greatly redefined. The institutions must be in control of the possible chaos that rapid, continuous changes can bring. Courses and certificates will be added, programs will be modified, stackable credentials will become the norm in order to deal with an ever and rapidly changing environment.

New methods of using the digital world that as yet have not been imagined will find their way into higher education. Faculty and staff will need to be continually reeducated and retrained. Informed, data-driven leadership will be needed to develop an active, future-focused institution.

Focus on Students

The focus on the student will become intense. Business, industry, and health organizations will need workforce members that are well educated, future-focused, and data-driven. The days of obtaining a job and holding it for 20–30 years until retirement are gone. The properly trained individual will face a work environment that requires that the members of the workforce be constantly upgraded in order to keep the business community competitive globally.

Focus on Faculty

The community college and university of the twenty-first century for the next few decades will find themselves in rapid flux, morph, and change constantly. It will require faculty who can adapt to change in their attitudes, focus, and expertise. Faculty will be needed who expect to be retrained and reeducated annually and perhaps quarterly, depending on the situation.

THE COMING TECHNOLOGIES

First on the horizon are autonomous vehicles and drones possibilities, but right alongside them are 3-D printing, the Internet of Things, personal robots, Bitcoin/Blockchain, and genome development. These examples are not coming 10 years in the future; they could impact higher education in the next three to five years.

Beyond those examples are artificial intelligence, nanotechnology, and quantum computing. All of these are visible now, but still on the blade of the metaphorical hockey stick. Determining exactly when they will begin the move up the shaft at this point is estimated to be in the 10–30 year timeframe. That estimate may be too far into the future, but from what can be seen today, it seems a logical estimate.

The argument as to what happens in the next 20–50 years is still very much undetermined, but it is critically important that those involved in community college and universities become aware of the possibilities. There are organizations and individuals internationally that are trying to determine where humanity is going in the next 20–50 year time period. (See chapter 9, Projections.)

The World Economic Forum spokesman Klaus Schwab, in his book *Shaping the Fourth Industrial Revolution*, states, "Creating a prosperous, inclusive and equitable Fourth Industrial Revolution for society and citizens means being conscious of the choices we make in technological systems which will inevitably impact economic, environmental and social systems" (p. 65).

CONCLUSION

This is a time in the history of mankind when tremendous changes brought on by a series of technologies will affect everyone on the planet. It is incumbent on those involved in higher education to be aware of the impending changes and work to make a beneficial world for all human beings.

PREPARING FOR THE FUTURE

- There are three big elephants in the room: artificial intelligence, nanotechnology, and quantum computing.

- Artificial intelligence uses silicon chips, which according to Moore's law states that the number of transistors on a chip doubles every 18 months, and which led to the fact that 30 billion transistors exist on a chip in 2018.
- IBM's Deep Blue computer was able to compete with Garry Kasparov, a champion chess player, and won the match in 1997.
- IBM's Watson computer played *Jeopardy* with the two best players, Ken Jennings and Brad Rutter, winning the competition in 2011.
- The Deep Blue and Watson computers are a known as narrow artificial intelligence as they were both limited in their abilities.
- The Watson computer was reprogrammed to work in the medical world with the disease of cancer and procedures to deal with it.
- Since Moore's law predicts doubling of computer power every 18 months, futurist Ray Kurzweil predicts that in the year 2045 a computer will exist that matches the mind of a human being, something called a Singularity.
- If the doubling process of computer power continues after artificial general intelligence is obtained, two to five years later artificial super intelligence will appear on the scene.
- In order to deal with artificial super intelligence, human beings may need to become cyber-humans with chips inserted in their brains and bodies.
- The second big elephant in the room is nanotechnology.
- In the future it will be possible to manufacture most anything starting at the atom level.
- Nanotechnology has been developing at a rather gradual rate due to the difficulties of working at the quantum level.
- Given successful development, nanotechnology could completely re-configure the world, the solar system, and perhaps the universe.
- The third big elephant in the room is quantum computing.
- A quantum computer would be phenomenally fast and make Moore's law look as if it were going in reverse.
- The fact that atoms exist in two places at once, a quandary impossible to understand, creates tremendous opportunities.
- A quantum computer uses atoms to create qubits that can be used in a computer. The ability of atoms to exist in two locations simultaneously allows for a phenomenally rapid speed of computing.
- Quantum computers are currently being developed in the United States, Canada, the United Kingdom, and other European countries.

- One country that seems very serious about developing quantum computing is China. The Chinese are constructing a four million square-foot facility at a cost of $10 billion, which is to be completed in 2020.
- For community colleges and universities to deal with quantum computing will take a complete change of mind and action.
- The technologies discussed in this book will redefine the business world, which in turn will transform higher education.
- Depending on the technology, some will affect higher education in the next three to five years, such as autonomous vehicles, 3-D printing, the Internet of Things, personal robots, and genome development.
- Other technologies, such as AI, nanotechnology, and quantum computing, will make their effect known over a much longer time period.
- Awareness of what is coming is absolutely crucial for success.

Chapter Four

Operations Internally and Externally

OPERATIONS INTERNALLY

Creating community colleges and universities that can deal with serial disruption caused by a number of developing technologies will take a good deal of analysis and a growth mind-set on the part of leaders and faculty. The educational institution will need to learn how to work in an exponential environment. The leaders will need to be aware of the changes that are coming. If the educational institutions desire to remain intact, they will have to do things differently. Business as usual will be old hat.

Truck Driving

Transportation is about to take a serious turn in the trucking business. Today there are approximately 3 million truck drivers in the United States who carry goods and equipment from one place to another. However, that entire industry will be tremendously impacted in the next 5–10 years as autonomous trucks come into their own. Self-driving trucks can transport goods and equipment from point A to point B without the assistance of a human driver (Hawkins, 2018).

Community College Instruction

When truck drivers are displaced, what are they to do? Since truck driving takes a specific set of skills that would not easily transfer to jobs in the digital world, community colleges are going to have to step in with serious retraining for these individuals. Because the jobs of the future will take a technology skill set, displaced truck drivers will most likely need to enroll in developmental studies to prepare for entrance into a technology-based program.

The extensive numbers of displaced individuals needing remedial education will place a financial strain on the community college. The funding from the state legislature will need to be increased or the federal government will need to provide colleges with grants to assist those needing basic training to be able to take advantage of digital jobs.

Increased Funding Needs

Explaining the increased financial need to state legislators and/or federal congressmen for displaced truckers will take data support and communication skills on the part of community college leaders. The basic argument most likely will be that the state legislature or Congress must help pay for the retraining needed by those who lost their jobs to autonomous trucks. If they are unable to do so, states and/or the federal government will end up paying basic living expenses for the displaced worker for an extended period of time.

It makes better sense to help individuals obtain the skills needed for the new jobs so they can support themselves rather than receiving state or federal support. In that way not only do the individuals affected not become wards of the state, but they also become workers who provide themselves and their families with a decent standard of living. In addition, they stabilize the tax base of the state and nation. Such an argument is not new, but in the case of displaced truckers and other workers displaced by technologies, it can be supported with data to help convince those in the political environs.

The trucking example could be multiplied by many other types of repetitive jobs that are taken over by personal robots, the Internet of Things, 3-D printing, autonomous cars, and genome development. Disruption in the world of work will be felt throughout the country. The community college and university will need to develop programs that suit the needs of the technologies used by business and industry. The disruptions caused by the twenty-first-century technologies will require program changes in the community colleges and universities along with increased funding for education and training of the displaced workforce.

Entrepreneurship Education

More individuals will attempt to begin new businesses than ever before. Both community colleges and universities will need to offer programs on entrepreneurship (Morgan, 2014). 3-D printing and the Internet of Things will create possibilities for new businesses that do not exist at present. Individuals who are interested in starting their own business will need the knowledge, support, and entrepreneurial skills that can be taught by institutions of higher education.

This is not a new idea. It has been used in the past. In Lynchburg, Virginia, a company which manufactured cell phones was located in a one million square foot facility. It employed over 1,000 people including a few hundred engineers. It was a flourishing company but ran upon hard times and had to shut down.

It turned out that some of the engineers did not want to move their families from Lynchburg and decided to work in an entrepreneurial fashion. They started a business in the wireless sector that they knew had potential in the state and beyond. In a few short years the business was flourishing. That kind of future-focused thinking used by those who can initiate a new company has the potential to grow significantly in the digital world.

Soft Skills

Further, the concept of soft skills as a requirement for the workforce is already a need expressed by the business community. Sometimes a business representative will state that most of what is needed by the business can be taught in company, but the soft skills needed are another story. Where does the individual learn soft skills? The community college and university will need to address that issue continuously.

Future jobs will demand more teamwork to get the job done. The day of the single person working in an isolated environment to develop what is needed for the business world is gone. Teams working together is already on the scene and the digital jobs of the future will only accelerate that need (Morgan, 2014). The answer to the need for expanded soft skill training may lie in the study of humanities.

Role of the Humanities

As businesses move rapidly into the digital world, the need for working in teams will increase dramatically. The academic area of the humanities can provide the foundation for developing the soft skills needed by the twenty-first-century workforce. Understanding communication skills, the psychological issues when working together, history, psychology, and literature will help the employee understand why people act as they do. Sociology will help the student to figure out how groups operate in the society. Humanities could become the bedrock of soft skills for future jobs in the business world.

Freelancing

Another approach to a career is freelancing. The freelance notion comes from the English author, Sir Walter Scott, who in his novel *Ivanhoe* wrote about knights who for various reasons had to make a living working independently on a contract basis for a variety of sources (Morgan, 2014). The freelance concept is very much alive today.

> According to a report by Intuit called the "Intuit 2020 Report: Twenty Trends that Shape the Next Decade," which was published in 2010, by 2020 around 40% of the U.S. workforce will be working as freelancers, temp workers, or contractors (some predict this number to be as high as 50%). This amounts to around 60 million people in the United States alone. (Morgan, 2014, p. 69)

And it is not just in the United States where this trend is evident. Other countries are moving down the same path. In the EU,

> More than half of all new jobs created . . . since 2010 have been through temporary contracts. Overall, among young people, 40% hold short term jobs without benefits. It is difficult to pay for full time employees and their accompanying full social benefits, so firms rely on temporary workers, who do not require costly benefits. (West, 2018, p. 81)

The Film Industry

When one attends a movie and is enthralled by what is seen and heard, it is usually not until the end of the film that a list of all those involved in the making of the production is reeled by in rapid succession. Usually the moviegoers are not paying much attention as they walk out from the theater. But if one takes the time to watch, it will soon be obvious that literally hundreds of people with various skills came together to make the movie a reality.

Today almost all those employed in the film industry, those names seen in the rollup at the end of the movie, are freelancers, from actors to graphic artists, from directors to cameramen. Many make a good living at it. The group is brought together to work for a limited period of time with each member providing certain functions that ultimately create the film. They need to have well-developed soft skills if they are interested in using their particular talents in the next movie.

Rather than being employed by a company, freelancers are employed in projects, like the production crew of a film where a variety of skills are needed. All those who work in the film industry are employed as subcontractors, a set of individuals needed to complete the project. Freelancing is a proven model to be used in the future when contract employment itself grows exponentially in many areas.

The community college and university could offer programs in how to successfully freelance in the upcoming technological world of work. Short-term contracts from days to months would become the norm. Serial learning would support those who are successful in this environment. Higher education institutions could assist those involved in freelancing to become successful in that endeavor.

Training Needed

How does one become successful in the freelance world of work? It would start with a good, basic education with a specialty in a particular field. Next, it would require networking with prospective employers. Further, it would require a high skill level and excellent interpersonal skills. Finally, it would require serial education in the field, most likely at the freelancer's expense. In addition, the individual must learn careful financial planning and budgeting (Morgan, 2014).

Freelancing could become a certificate or associate degree program in the community college environment. Teaching students the basics of freelancing is a start. Finding internships for a freelance student could be developed. Further instruction in networking and making contacts could be provided. It would seem to be a natural direction for the community college to take when a growing percentage of the workforce will use freelancing as way of making a living.

My daughter graduated from college with a degree in media studies. She started her career in a local South Carolina TV station, but after about a year she decided she wanted more. She moved to the Los Angeles area, because of the sheer size of the market. She worked for a graphics company for about a year and then phoned me to ask if she should consider going freelance. I told her if freelancing did not work out, she could always go back to work for a media company.

That was over 25 years ago. As a result of her success in freelancing in the television arena, she have been all over the world with a rather amazing lifestyle. Although she is an anecdotal example, working as a contract person has worked well for her. Her success over the years demonstrates that if the freelancing work style becomes a normal way to make a living, it could be done successfully.

The Faculty in the Digital World

On the other side of the training coin is the faculty. They will have to bring a growth mind-set to their positions. Continual training and re-training, education and reeducation will become the norm for successful faculty. The search for faculty will no longer focus only on academic credentials, which will be a foundation of the skill set needed, but beyond credentials will be the need for faculty members who are aware of technology, willing to be retrained as needed, and understand the how critical it is to be continually reeducated.

Continuing Education

In the community college world, training for short-term work has been around for decades. It is often found in a division of the college called Continuing Education or Workforce Development. What is going on there is immediate reaction to business and community needs. The division develops short courses as well as lengthy training programs to meet the direct needs of an organization in the community. In the future the successful years of experience in providing training for businesses may be of great assistance to the community college as it deals with a rapidly changing technological world.

Being well educated in one topic or discipline will no longer be all that is needed. It will provide a foundation for teaching expertise, but the ability to move from one area to the next will become more important if the faculty member wants continued employment and the institution desires to remain viable. It may mean going back to school for specific learning annually or more often, which could develop into a set of stacked credentials.

In other words, the successful faculty members of the future will be those who are foundationally well-versed in education and are able and willing to be reeducated and retrained often for the benefit of students, the businesses, the college, and themselves. Twentieth-century faculty patterns will be left behind and soon forgotten.

Career Counselors in the Digital World

Circling back to the beginning of this chapter, how does the community college or university deal with the students in the future who come to the college looking for a new start on their career? This is the point where career counseling will become critically important. Helping displaced workers and assisting the recent high school graduates prepare for a successful career to make a decent standard of living will take an entirely new approach.

The career counselors will need to be well informed as to what is going on in the world of technology in terms of existing positions, what developments are under way, and where things are likely to go in the future. It will be critical that the counselor imbue the idea in the student that enrolling in a community college or university is only a beginning; it is like being in the starting blocks of a long triathlon that goes in many directions that demands a variety of skills.

The student will need to understand that they will receive training and education that will get them a job, but that job may only last for only a year or two. It will be necessary on their part to constantly analyze where the business is going and what will be needed in the future to help keep it successful.

While holding one position, the individual will need to be preparing for the next one, which might be in the same company or elsewhere. There is the possibility that constant retraining could be supported by the business involved. However, training supported by the individual is another more likely method.

Students will find themselves in serial training and retraining, holding a position for some period of time, watching it evaporate, and moving on to the next one. The career counselor will need to make sure the potential student understands the method of making a living that involves a string of short-term positions with continual retraining. The counselor will have to imbue the importance of constant research on the part of the student in order to be able to find the path to the next job.

Students in the Digital World

The community college and the university will need to inculcate in the minds of students the notion that completing a program and graduating only one time, as in the past, is no longer enough. Going back to higher education for serial retraining and, in many cases, moving into entirely new fields requiring totally different training and education, will become the new norm. It will become an expectation on the part of students, businesses, government, community colleges, and universities.

This rapidly changing world of work will undoubtedly create stress on the part of the student. It is critical that the community college and the university educate students on how to deal with stress that they will most likely experience. The digital world is not anything like the agricultural world of the nineteenth century or the manufacturing world of the twentieth century. Students will need to be aware of what is coming and taught the appropriate ways of dealing with it.

Businesses in the Digital World

Businesses will be looking for employees who understand the digital world, the exponential changes that most likely will take place, and the ability to learn and relearn repeatedly (West, 2018). Although that may sound difficult, it will be critical to the success of businesses and the workforce. The business will need to operate at the front edge of what is going on in order to compete globally. Members of the workforce will need to understand and accept that situation.

From the perspective of the twentieth century, the working world of the twenty-first century will appear chaotic, full of new rules, and blurring in its speed. It will be up to the individual to see the patterns that lead to success in life. The farmers who came to the city in the nineteenth and twentieth centuries figured it out; the current workforce moving into the digital world will have do the same. The community college and university can be of inestimable help for those experiencing the changes in the twenty-first century.

The community college and the university in the twenty-first century will morph and transform in order to properly and appropriately serve the students, businesses, and economic development. Lessons can always be learned from the past, but using past models to operate successfully in the future has the potential of leading to failure for all concerned.

OPERATIONS EXTERNALLY

The community college and the university are not standalone organizations. Both are connected in different ways to the business community. Whereas the community college is part of the local business community, the university stretches out to the state, regional, national, and global environment. The important point is that neither of the institutions is an island onto itself; both are integral parts of the business world.

Universities

Historically, the land grant university, supported financially at the federal level, began with the passage of the Morrill Act in 1862 during the Lincoln administration. The universities were designed to serve the agricultural, science, military science, and engineering training needs. Today all states have a university that can be traced back to the land grant legislation. Those universities as well as others, state and private, have served the theoretical and practical scientific needs of the nineteenth and twentieth centuries. Today they continue to play an important role in higher education in the United States.

Community Colleges

Community colleges trace their history back to the vision of the founding president of the University of Chicago, Dr. William Rainey Harper, who in 1895 initiated what became the junior college, which in turn morphed into the community college in the 1960s (Cohen et al., 2014). The community college provides its service area with practical training for the local business community in addition to serving students with college transfer programs for those who desire to continue on to the university. Beyond those two functions, the community colleges usually work in a close support role with local economic development initiatives.

Land grant universities and community colleges provide education and training on the practical, hands-on level used by business, industry, and health organizations. Both types of institutions have developed connections and partnerships with the business community, which places them in an excellent position to remain successful and viable on the future technological stage.

SERIAL EDUCATION

The twenty-first-century technologies will demand a close working relationship between the business community and higher education. Serial education and training will become a vital part of the successful business and the members of the workforce. In turn, serial education will keep the community college and university viable (Meister et al., 2017). Partnerships between the two will become critical to their survival. A symbiotic relationship will develop far beyond anything seen in the past. The business world and higher education will not be able to survive without the other.

The universities will most likely support and assist the business community as they become further involved with specific technologies. The university will be in a position to develop the algorithms and software the businesses will use. Further, the universities and businesses will be at the forefront of the development of the technologies involved.

The community colleges will partner with the business community to help continuously train and retrain their workforces. The close relationship between community colleges and the business community will be very valuable as they move together into the twenty-first century. Their relationship will grow and develop significantly as they support students, the workforce, and the community.

The university and the community college will need to provide education leading to degrees in business that managers will need in the exponential organization of the future. The businesses will need specifically educated and trained individuals to operate successfully. Both types of educational institutions will feel the demand made by the business community. Working together, the community college, the university, and the businesses will create success for all concerned.

HIGHER EDUCATION PARTNERSHIPS

In addition, partnerships between community colleges and universities will proliferate as well. Both members of the higher education community will understand the value of providing an interfaced method of developing solutions to the needs of the business community and providing the training for the workforce. Both will understand the need to be continuously updated on the development of the technologies. Both will need to work shoulder-to-shoulder in harmony to support the business community.

WORKFORCE OF THE FUTURE

On the part of some futurists, it is thought that there will not be enough jobs to go around in the future (Clifton, 2011). However, one needs only to hark back to the mid-1980s with the advent of the personal computer. At that time doomsday prognosticators predicted that entire strata of clerical workers would be displaced by the computer. However, they were not. Instead they learned to provide new and better services that improved the operation of both educational institutions and businesses.

There is the possibility that the job loss created by the twenty-first-century technologies may not be nearly as great as some forecast. Although it can be predicted that many jobs which exist in today's working world will be deleted, it is just as possible that new jobs will replace many of them. There is also the potential that many of the current jobs will expand in capability making for a more efficient and effective workplace.

Partnerships between Higher Education and Businesses

Whichever the case, it will be incumbent upon the community college and the university to continually operate hand-in-hand with the business world. To be of the most value to students and the business community, it is critical that the educational institutions understand the developments in the AI environment and the many other technologies in existence. Operating in a continuous updating mode will be critical to the higher education institutions, the business community, and the students.

It is extremely helpful that community colleges have traditionally worked with the business community dating back to the 1920s (Witt et al., 1994). That business/community college relationship creates a solid foundation to build on for the technological world of the twenty-first century. Many universities have done the same over the years, which will put them in a strong position for even more integrated work with business community.

It appears that the technologies already in existence and those to be developed in the future will require a symbiotic relationship between the business community and higher education to serve the best interests of all concerned. That would create an extremely significant change in the mission and vision of higher education. It is something that will soon be on the table for discussion and action in the near future.

CONCLUSION

Internally and externally, the community college and the university will operate very differently in the coming decades than they do today. The institutions of higher education that succeed will find ways to deal with exponential change. The best way to do that will be to operate in an exponential manner of awareness, research, planning, and action, which will be discussed later in this book.

PREPARING FOR THE FUTURE

- In the near future educational institutions will need to learn how to work in an exponential environment.
- The trucking industry will be seriously impacted by the autonomous truck.
- Displaced truck drivers will need to learn skills for a totally different career.
- At the community college level remedial education will need to be expanded, which will cause serious financial strain.
- Working with state legislators and congressmen will take data and communication skills to secure additional funding.
- It should be in the best interest of governmental officials to assist displaced workers to obtain the new skills needed for the digital world.
- Disruption in many repetitive jobs, caused by the use of personal robots and other technologies, will impact the world of work throughout the country.
- Many displaced individuals may look to start their own business. As a result community colleges and universities will have opportunities to teach entrepreneurship.
- Soft skills on the part of employees will become more critical as work in the digital world will demand teamwork.
- The humanities areas that already exist in community colleges and universities could do much to fill the soft skills void.
- Freelancing is another career choice that could be made by many. Teaching how this is done could become a program offering in community colleges and universities.
- The film industry is an excellent example of how freelancing works successfully.
- A number of skills need to be taught for the individual who wishes to be successful in the freelance world of work.

- Faculty in community colleges and universities will have to bring a growth mindset to their position and be prepared to go through continual retraining and reeducation to meet the needs of the institution.
- Continuing education, which has been an active part of community colleges for decades, will be a model for developing training and education for continually changing skills.
- Career counselors will become another critical component of the community college and university student services area.
- Counselors will need to be trained to work with students, explaining that any training or education received at the institution may be useful for a job for as little as one year but most likely not much longer than two or three.
- Serial training and retraining will become the norm.
- Students will need to learn that graduating only one time, as in the past, is no longer sufficient.
- The rapidly changing world of work will undoubtedly create stress on the part of the student. They will need to learn how to deal with stress successfully.
- The business world will be looking for employees to understand the rapid changes that take place in the digital world.
- The working world of the twenty-first century will appear chaotic and it will be up to the individual to find the patterns that lead to success.
- Community colleges and universities will be working together closely with the business community.
- Serial education and training will become a vital part of the successful business and its employees.
- The university and community college provide education and training that leads to success in the exponential organization of the future.
- Partnerships between community colleges and universities will proliferate.
- At this point it is hard to say whether there will be not enough jobs or too many in the future. Most likely jobs will be very different from those of today.
- Community colleges and universities will operate continually hand-in-hand with the business world.
- Internally and externally the community college and the university will transform into organizations quite different from those of today.

Chapter Five

Unaffected Occupations

The effects of the era of serial disruptions, which are widespread and powerful, will create a phenomenal amount of change in the higher education, the workforce, and the middle class. Students will have to learn and understand that with a digital world comes extreme, rapid, continual change.

However, there are a number of occupations that will not be significantly affected by the exponential development of technologies. These occupations include sports, artists, musicians, dancers, actors, clergy, nurses, physicians, and most likely plumbers, electricians, HVAC technicians, and welders.

In addition, Darrell West, in his book *The Future of Work* (2018), points out other occupations that most likely will not be affected by technology, such as, "recreational therapists, mechanic supervisors, emergency management directors, mental health social workers, audiologists, occupational therapists, health care social workers, oral surgeons, supervisors of firefighters, and dietitians" (p. 70).

SPORTS

It is hard to imagine robots taking over the sport of baseball. If all of the robot baseball players were able to play perfect games all the time, the interest in the game would die off rather quickly. Who would care how well robots play? It would be boring to watch them. And what about football? If the robot quarterback could always hit the receiver successfully because it could jump 10 feet in the air and throw a perfect pass, how long would interest in the game continue? Again, boredom would soon set in.

Basketball with robots? Who would want to watch robots who could always swish the ball through the net even from the opposite end of the court? What about the robot golfer who could always hit the ball precisely where it needed to go every time? Or the tennis robot which could place the ball exactly in the right place repeatedly? How about the robot soccer players who could play without errors? Sports is most likely an area that will remain in the hands of human players.

Robots may provide supportive tasks, but the actual playing of the sports that individuals globally know and love most likely would not happen. Sports is an occupation that is not repetitive and simple. The thinking, creative approaches, and human physical stamina in combination play a big part in what makes the game fascinating to the person in the stands or along the fairway.

The art world is another area that most likely the robot or the computer will have limited effect upon. At present a computer with a well-designed algorithm can write a play-by-play description of a baseball game that is close to as good as anything a professional press writer can do. That ability rests on the fact that describing a baseball game is relatively repetitive (Ford, 2015).

On the other hand, writing a novel, one that would enthrall human beings, seems at this point in time to be a long shot at best for a robot. The artist using oil paint is another that seems to be a human occupation. Robots have already tried painting, but most likely they will remain in second place.

MUSICIANS

Are music and musicians on the chopping block only to be replaced by robots who design music and play it on today's instruments? Another long shot, but perhaps more possible than other artists. A symphony may be a possibility, but good jazz music full of innovation, probably not.

Who would be attracted to watch a ballet of robots who did everything perfectly? That would quickly fall into the category of boredom. Most likely the reason performing artists attract an audience is that they are human beings who have learned to do something that most humans cannot accomplish. When they do it extremely well, the audience is impressed and interested because they know that most humans cannot perform the intricate moves. A ballerina robot? Probably not.

THE FILM INDUSTRY

What about the movies, TV shows, and those who play roles in making them come to life? Are actors, playwrights, directors, and the myriad of support personnel going to be replaced by robots? Seems unlikely or if they do, who will be interested in watching them? Other robots? Most likely not human beings.

THE TRADES

In addition, it is hard to envision that plumbers, electricians, HVAC technicians, welders, firefighters, and first responders would all disappear to be replaced by robots. There are probably many more possibilities that cannot be robotized that will become obvious as days move into months and years of the technology disruptions.

The occupations that do not seem to be able to be taken over by computers or robots may become a mainstay in the offerings of higher education. Perhaps more potential students would be interested in the sports, the arts, the media, or technical fields than are now, an indirect effect of technology.

Further, will there be new occupations that are created by the technologies that can only be accomplished by humans, technology enhanced humans, or teams of humans (enhanced or not) and robots? Most likely those will appear on the scene and provide the future workforce with jobs we have a hard time envisioning today.

NEW OCCUPATIONS

The future will be filled with unanticipated, totally different occupations than what are known today. Trying to figure out what suits humans and what is better done by robots will lead to data and serious discussions in the future.

There is always the possibility that human beings could be enhanced by chips inserted into their bodies and brains that will give them an equal playing field with computers and robots. This is an area that has not been investigated or researched much at this point in time. At least one writer sees it as a very logical way for humans to remain vital and sustainable in the future (Barfield, 2015). He points out that we are already using implants of various types from teeth to hip replacements that just two generations back were not even possibilities.

3-D printing could become the pathway for success in this regard. Scientists are already experimenting with body organs like lungs and livers. How far down the road is upgrading the brain itself for increasingly better results? Another method could be CRISPER/Cas9, which could revise the genome to keep humans not only up to par, but perhaps place them far in advance of the computer. And what about the quantum world? Is there a possibility there to improve the human mind that we have not even imagined?

Do not forget that looking into the future is often blurred by the experiences of the past. It is hard to see past what has been experienced. Further, the understanding of everything is limited by the five senses combined with Newton's laws, which literally force understanding to remain within fixed parameters. The imagination is the way out of that dilemma and it will have to be used extensively as the twenty-first century moves ahead into the future.

CONCLUSION

However, once started down the new world of technologies, there is no coming back. Learning to adapt will become the key to existence, a key that was discovered by Charles Darwin, which became the theory of evolution. Adapting will become as common as breathing in the future of exponential change created by technologies. Evolution will morph into something better described as serial revolution. It will be critical to be prepared for that concept in the technological world.

PREPARING FOR THE FUTURE

- Although serial disruption will affect many repetitive jobs in the near future, there are some occupations which most likely will not be significantly affected by the development of technologies.
- Most likely robots will not take over the sports of baseball, basketball, golf, tennis, or soccer.
- The art world is another area that most likely robots or computers will have limited effect on.
- Some areas of music may be affected by the computer, but jazz music, which is full of innovation, will probably not be affected.
- Ballet is another art form that most likely will not be affected by robots.
- Most of the trades such as plumbers, electricians, air-conditioning technicians, welders, and firefighters most likely will not be replaced by robots.
- Occupations where computers and robots will most likely not be able to replace human beings may become the centerpiece of offerings in higher education.
- In the future there will be many unanticipated, totally different occupations that are not known today.
- In the future human beings may very well be enhanced by chips inserted into their brains and bodies to put them on an equal playing field with computers and robots.
- Trying to see into the future is often blurred by experiences of the past because it is hard to understand beyond what has been experienced.
- Learning to adapt will be the key to existence.

Chapter Six

Financial Planning

In the next decades the community college and the university will need considerable funding to keep up with the development of the technologies as they impact the students, faculty, facilities, equipment, administration, business community, and workforce. As the technology develops in an exponential manner, both the community college and the university will need to modify their operations in a variety of ways. A new paradigm of business, work, and making a living will arrive.

BUSINESS COMMUNITY

Since the business community will rapidly become engaged with the new technologies in order to remain internationally competitive, it will look to the community college and the university as organizations which can help and support them. Making sure they can meet the demands of business, educational institutions will have to adapt. No other choice will exist.

STUDENTS

Students will need to be carefully counseled in terms of the meaning of exponential change and how it will affect their ability to make a living during their lifetimes. There will be many pathways a students can follow, all of which will require an attitude of being ready to continuously learn and relearn as jobs come and go more rapidly.

COUNSELORS

The kinds of professionals it will take in the counseling department of the institution will need considerably different education to deal with those recruited as students. Counselors will need to understand the future of work that the technologies will bring.

FACULTY

In the digital world the specific field the faculty member studied will need to be augmented by an acceptance of the fact that the mid-twenty-first-century workforce demands will mean morphing from a single-discipline specialist to a multi-discipline generalist.

FACILITIES

Facilities in an exponential community college or university will need to be designed in such a way that they can be easily modified from training needed for one technology to that needed for another. Since there will be a continual series of disruptions, the serial learning space, whether class-rooms or labs, will become commonplace.

EQUIPMENT

Since the technologies will change, develop, and intertwine with each other to best serve the business community, community colleges and universities must be ready to obtain the most up-to-date equipment that will be needed for education and training.

ADMINISTRATION

There will be a need for college and university administrators to fully understand the concept of an exponential organization of higher education. A sincere and well-developed growth mindset will be critical to the success of administrators and the institutions they lead.

FINANCING

State and Federal

Obtaining the financing to keep community colleges and universities solvent will become a daunting activity. It will be in the best interest of state and the federal government to continue to support public community colleges and public universities. Since both the state and federal government need a strong, solid tax base to exist, most likely both will continue to support community colleges and the universities as long as the institutions work hand-in-hand with the business community.

The symbiotic relationship between higher education and the business community will help to support funding from legislative and congressional sources. Most politicians understand the need for a flourishing economy and if community colleges and universities are working to make that a reality, requesting funding from state and federal sources becomes more reasonable.

STUDENT TUITION AND FEES

There are always student tuition and fees, which provide significant revenue by themselves. Since the community college and university will be working so closely with the business community, it would be an easy move to ask the involved members of the business community to financially support the costs of a student attending the institution. This could be connected to a number of years the student would have to work at the business involved.

ALTERNATIVE FUND-RAISING

Fund-raising from sources outside of state and federal governments will become extremely important to community colleges and universities. One source both types of institutions will look to is the business community. Since it is in the best interest of the business to work with community colleges and universities to provide the workforce, they will be in excellent place for both types of institutions to begin. Expanding funding from that source may come relatively easy since it is in the best interest of both organizations.

Further, the 501.c.3 Foundations of community colleges and universities could purchase businesses themselves in order to use the profit to help sustain the institutions. This type of fund-raising is already being used in a small number of institutions, but it could be expanded considerably in the future.

 In other words, the financial revenue of the institution of higher education in the future may change to something very unlike than that experienced in the twentieth century and the early twenty-first. Since the digital world is very different from the analog world, the chances are that both the business community and higher education will morph into forms that currently can only be imagined.

CONCLUSION

Leadership in the community college and the university will soon be faced with changes coming at them from every side. To be successful in the digital world will take understanding of the situation, creative approaches to the challenges, and inventive methods of making the institution viable, successful, and secure. This new paradigm is not for the faint of heart, but is a challenge that faces educational leaders in the near future, but there is no reason to believe it cannot be handled successfully by those who really care.

PREPARING FOR THE FUTURE

- Funding for the community college and the university will be extremely critical in the future.
- Businesses will be looking to the community college and the university as institutions who can support and help them.

- Students will need appropriate, extensive counseling in terms of their careers.
- Counselors will need to understand the future of work that the technologies will bring.
- Faculty will need to be continually upgrading their skills to become multi-disciplined generalists.
- Facilities will need to be easily modified to meet the training needs from one technology to another.
- Equipment, which will need to be state-of-the-art, will become a major expense for the college.
- Administrators will need to fully understand the concept of the exponential organization.
- Financing for community college and university solvency will be difficult at best.
- Student tuition and fees will remain a mainstay of revenue for both types of institutions.
- Fund-raising from alternative sources will become critical.
- Foundations of community colleges and universities may purchase or develop businesses to help sustain the institutions.
- Expect that the financial situation of higher education in the future will be different from today.
- What faces the administrators in the future is not for the faint of heart; however, there is no reason to believe it cannot be handled successfully.

Chapter Seven

Exponential Administration

In a technological world developing at an exponential pace that is creating serial disruptions, community colleges and universities will need leaders who can operate in futuristic ways with a growth mind-set in order deal with the impacts the technologies will have on their institutions. Success in an era of serial disruptions will require educational leaders to think in an exponential manner. Successful previous models of administration will need to be significantly modified, or most likely replaced. Much of what worked so well for leaders in the twentieth century will not meet the leadership needs in the twenty-first.

Unlearn/Relearn

To a large extent, previous ways of doing things will need to be unlearned. The community college and university will need to reeducate presidents, vice presidents, deans, and department chairs. They are the leaders who must become aware of the twenty-first-century technologies. They must research how the developing technologies will affect their respective institutions. They must plan how to deal with the changes for the benefit of students, faculty/staff, and the business community. Finally, they must take appropriate actions to deal with the impacts of technologies. Unlearning, relearning, and reeducation will be the new norm.

Graduate Programs

Master degree and doctoral programs for prospective community college and university leaders will need to be extensively revised in order to be of assistance to future administrators. To be successful in digital world, the upcoming leaders will need to thoroughly understand what they will be facing. They will need to be imbued with an extensive knowledge of the exponential technologies. Serious study will be required.

In addition, they will need to understand the importance of continual research into those technologies as they develop along the blade of the metaphorical hockey stick. Knowing when the gradual development becomes exponential in speed and distribution will be critical to the success of the institution, administration, faculty, and students.

Faculty and staff will need to be continuously upgraded. Program offerings will need to be added and deleted. Equipment and technology will need to be state-of-the-art. Facilities will need to be flexible. It will take highly talented leaders, faculty, and staff to keep the community college and the university successful and beneficial to all concerned. Even the mission and vision will need to be redesigned.

For some in leadership this will be a workable transition; for others, the serial disruptions may cause them to try to hold back the tide before they understand the consequences. But sooner rather than later they will come to the conclusion that either they become reeducated to deal with the technological advances or they must leave the institutions they lead.

For those who stay, a change in mind-set to work within the new paradigm will be necessary. For those who join the institutions, the new mind-set will need to be accepted and pursued. That mind-set will begin with an acceptance of continuous, rapid change and growth.

LEADERSHIP IN AN EXPONENTIAL ENVIRONMENT

According to the noted psychologist Dr. Carol Dweck of Stanford University, a growth mind-set is defined as being open to change and being willing to grow and develop to deal with it (2006). A growth mind-set will be critical to success for the leaders of community colleges and universities in the future. Making the changes needed for success in the future may seem like an almost impossible task; however, impossibilities that have faced leaders in the past were often turned on their head and successes were created.

Recall the Carthaginian general, Hannibal Barca, who lived two hundred years before Christ, when he stood observing the Alps, with an army of 50,000 troops and 37 elephants behind him. They had followed and fought for him over hundreds of miles from the northern coast of Africa and through what is now Spain. Hannibal was told that trying to cross the mountain range was not only foolhardy, but totally impossible. The enemy was waiting for them all along the trail up the mountain. If, by quirk of good luck, he managed to get himself, his army, and the elephants to the top, there was no pathway down the other side.

Hannibal is reported to have said, "We will find a way or make one." His army fought off the enemy on the way up the mountain. When they got to the top, there was no way down the other side. Apparently they set fires on the other side of the mountain, which cracked the rocks with the heat and created a path down the other side. In 15 days he and his army, were down on the other side, resting and waiting for the Roman army. When the Roman army appeared, they were slaughtered in proportions of ten Roman soldiers to every one of Hannibal's men (Lancel, 1998).

Growth Mind-Set

The foundation of the exponential executive is growth mind-set, one that is constantly future-focused and acceptant of growth and change (Dweck, 2006). The status quo, the existing state of affairs, will not work in the exponentially developing technological world. Maybe a new phrase to use might be *novo quo*, that is, the change state of affairs. Whatever the term, exponential technologies will demand that leaders deal with change successfully for all concerned.

THE ARPAC PROCESS

The question is, how is that done? What develops an exponential leader who creates an exponential institution of higher education? Many ways will probably be tried, some successful, others discarded. From the point of view of today, a suggested method would be a five-part process: Awareness, Research, Planning, Action, and Caring (ARPAC). Each step will be critical to success and the entire process must be used repeatedly as exponential technologies develop rapidly on various pathways.

Awareness

The first step of the ARPAC process is awareness. The leaders must be aware of all the technologies developing in the twenty-first century. They must understand that each is developing in an exponential manner along the metaphorical hockey stick blade to its shaft. The technologies will develop in what appears to be a gradual manner before suddenly taking off in extreme, rapid change. That gradual to exponential pattern will be seen again and again. It must be understood as the new norm in order to be dealt with successfully.

Leaders will need to view the technologies from a crow's nest perspective as well as from an up-close-and-personal acquaintance. Merely knowing the technologies exist is only a beginning. Awareness must lead to continuous research. The technologies involved do not come into existence and stop. Rather, they come into existence and impact individuals, society, and culture, just as past technologies have, only now at a much faster velocity.

Discovery must become a daily function of the leader. Looking in various directions to determine what is literally coming at the institution must become the norm, if there is any possibility of success as an institution of higher education in the twenty-first century. It will take constant vigilance on the part of the leaders.

Some may argue that educational leaders have been using awareness of change for decades. That may be true, but the awareness was of technologies developing in a linear manner. Linear development was last century's method. In an exponential digital world, thinking linearly will leave the leader and the institution in the dust. Awareness of the fact that twenty-first-century technologies develop in an exponential manner is what the current century will demand.

Research

The second step in the process is continuous, ongoing research. It will be critical to constantly follow each technology identified as to when it will impact the institution. This is not an annual event, as waiting that long may put the institution so far behind that it cannot catch up. It must be ongoing, with regular meetings for the leaders and faculty to be updated with information garnered from a wide variety of internal and external sources. Discussion meetings may need to take place weekly, monthly, quarterly, and annually depending on the development of the specific technology involved.

Both community colleges and universities should set up research committees to constantly trace the development of specific technologies. These committees could be made up of a cross section of employees with the charge that all members will continually research and be on the lookout for how the technology involved is developing and when it will impact the institution, students, faculty, staff, and administration.

The institution should consider appointing a vice president to coordinate the research and reports of the committees. Administrators at the dean level might be assigned to each of committees as facilitators to follow up on the researching and reporting. This may sound like extra time and effort. For certain it is, but it will be necessary if the institution is to remain viable in a world of technologies that are developing exponentially.

The administration of the institution should schedule regular, periodic meetings of the entire faculty and staff to hear the reports of the committees. If the technology is progressing along the blade of the hockey stick in a slow manner, perhaps like nanotechnology, longer time periods between meetings would be used. If the technology is moving more quickly, such as 3-D printing and genome development toward the shaft of the hockey stick, meetings will need to be held more often.

The idea behind the committees and the periodic reports is that they will provide updates to help everyone in the institution understand the progress of the technology. Only with continuously updated information and data can the institution itself expect to remain in a viable, successful position. In other words, everyone in the community college or the university must be a part of the process of determining what is going to impact the institution and when it will happen.

The notion that one can wait and see what happens and then make a move is no longer valid. The idea that one institution can follow another's lead is procrastination that could lead to serious problems. The community college and the university must make every effort to be ahead of the curve rather than trying to follow up from behind.

In the twentieth century the fast-follow pursuit of change worked well because the technology involved developed at a linear rate. In the twenty-first century, the institution must be prepared to deal with change before it occurs. To wait and see is a path that will lead the institution toward disaster.

If the leaders are fully aware of what is happening as a result of continuous research, they will able to make appropriate decisions. Decisions concerning technological developments may have to be made often during a fiscal year. The hockey stick is only a metaphor to describe what will be needed, how much will be needed, and how fast it will be needed. Taking all that into consideration is the responsibility of those leading the institution.

Research into the exponential development of technologies that lead to specific actions taken by the community college and the university is absolutely critical. Although the institutions may begin with current faculty and administrators to accomplish the research and reporting, in the near future the institutions may need to hire individuals to lead those tasks. The president, vice presidents, and the board members of the college will need to make rapid decisions as to the direction of the institution often on monthly, quarterly, and annual bases.

In terms of technology, at this point in time it is obvious that a community college should be researching 3-D printing, autonomous vehicles and drones, the Internet of Things, and genome development as they are getting close to leaving linear development behind and moving to exponential development. The community college and the university must be fully informed through research so that the leaders of the institution can take action needed to deal with the rapid, upcoming changes.

The research can help the university decide what the technologies will need in terms of engineering programs and courses. Engineering will become a platform for the development of some of the technologies. Research will help the community colleges decide what courses will be needed for the local business community, what training will be needed for faculty, what equipment will be needed for the training, and how the equipment can be obtained. Continual research will become a mainstay of the university and the community college.

In the digital world, one breakthough will lead to another. In addition, two technologies may interface and create a new technology that will need attention as well. Waiting see what happens and trying to understand it when it does will put higher education institutions in a no-win position.

The committees researching technological development in each institution of higher education will provide the community college and the university with the information and data they will need to stay abreast of the education, training, and workforce needs no matter whether the institution is dealing with a single technology, or two, or more.

Planning

The third step is planning. With the research data in hand, the community college and university executives must be analytical and ready to plan future directions in a timely manner. Even with a growth mind-set and a great deal of data and updating coming in regularly, it is critical to handle the information and data in a timely, well-thought-out manner.

Guesswork and gut feelings will not keep the institution on the right track. Data analytics will. Facts, data, and correct information will need to be analyzed to support the leaders in making the right decisions within logical time frames. Planning what actions should be taken will result from the analysis. It must be completed in a rapid, accurate manner.

Again, the community college and the university will want to create specific committees to analyze the data and information the research committees are discovering. A data analysis committee could be the team that makes recommendations to the institution's leadership as to what kind of planning is needed to deal with an impending change in the technology. Being prepared in a timely manner will make all the difference between success and failure.

Action

Fourth, the leaders in community colleges and senior institutions of higher education will need to take appropriate and accurate action. The actions could lead to new program development in rapid order, deletion of programs no longer needed, quick updating of faculty to deal with the development of the technologies, and continual modifications of the planning. To keep up with the exponential speed of the changes the technologies will take, the leaders of higher education will need to learn how to deal with the tsunami-like changes that might hit them from all sides.

The changes will need to be completed in the fastest time period possible. Technology waits for no one. Technology developing on the shaft of the hockey stick will in the blink of eye turn everything onto new pathways. The community college and the university must be continually prepared to take action as needed and when needed.

Yearlong decision making will not be sufficient. Decisions in time periods of days and weeks will become the norm. Leaders with a growth mind-set will have a chance of keeping up and remaining successful for all concerned; others, stuck in the status quo, will be left behind in the dust.

Caring

Finally, the exponential executives must care about the institution, its students, its faculty/staff, the business community, and those in charge of economic development. Caring about the college or university must take priority over the career interests of the leader. No longer will successful institutions of higher education exist at the whims and gut feelings of the leadership.

In order to make the future institution of higher education work successfully, it will need to be led by individuals who really care about the mission and vision of the institution. The successful leader will need continuous assistance and support from internal and external sources.

Awareness, research, planning, action, and caring (ARPAC), all of which rest on the foundation of a growth mind-set, are the characteristics needed by successful presidents, vice presidents, deans, department chairs, and faculty. The mind-set of the leadership team will make all the difference as to whether the community college or university succeeds or fails in the twenty-first century. Leaders will need to work together continuously redesigning the college environment to remain shoulder-to-shoulder with the needs of the business community, health organizations, and economic development initiatives.

THE ROLE OF THE COMMUNITY COLLEGE

All of the technologies will make significant, ongoing changes and modifications that will be used by local business, industry, and health organizations. The workforce of local businesses will need continual training to remain in a globally competitive position.

This situation will put a great deal of stress on the community college to remain a viable training organization. First, the community college will need to be well-informed on the upcoming changes. Second, the college will need to provide training to upgrade the faculty when needed. Third, using its continuously updated faculty, the college will need to offer courses and programs to retrain the workforce of the business. Finally, the college will need to find financial sources to obtain state-of-the-art equipment and appropriate facilities.

The community college may make extensive use of its Continuing Education Division to meet any short-term training needs and its Academic Affairs Division to develop certificate and degree programs where extensive retraining is necessary. In other words, the community college will be in the perfect position to provide the continual upgrade training needed by the business community.

To be successful in meeting this continual demand will mean significant input on technology developments, formal and informal research into the business needs, and a shoulder-to-shoulder working relationship with the businesses involved. It will become incumbent on all concerned to operate in a symbiotic manner. To do less will invite disaster. The community colleges will work directly with the business and health community providing them with workforce training and upgrades as needed, which will come much more often than experienced in the past.

THE ROLE OF THE UNIVERSITY

The university will be working on a higher level, helping to develop the changes needed to make the business community successful. The university will need well-developed research into the business community to ascertain its needs. It should be assisting in developing the technologies needed by the businesses in the region and state. Exponential leadership will be needed at the university level to proceed slightly ahead of the businesses.

To be successful in the twenty-first century, universities will find themselves working closer with business and health organizations at the state and regional level to develop existing and new technologies to keep the businesses up-to-date and globally competitive.

THE LEADERSHIP ROLE

When leading a community college or university in a world with technologies developing exponentially, how does the leader help the institution to transform from one that thinks and acts linearly to one that operates exponentially? The president and others in leadership will need to take the following steps to keep the institution viable and capable of dealing with the rapid change mode.

STEP ONE

The president should begin with the institution's administrators. This team of leaders from vice president to department chair need to become aware of which technologies are developing exponentially that will have a direct impact on the institution. Research will be critical; data will be needed for accurate decision making and ultimate actions.

The learning process may take multiple-day conferences to understand the leadership situation in general. Further, the institution may need to send appropriate administrators to national conferences outside of education to learn more about the technologies involved and best practices to deal with them. The business world is constantly investigating what technologies can best support them in the globally competitive world. To get behind the curve is to go out of business. CEOs know that and work to keep themselves and their organizations at the front edge of developments.

The entire administrative group of the community college and the university must be keyed in to the changes the technologies will make on the institution involved. Since the technologies will change the operation of the institution, all in leadership positions must be working together to make certain that the institution can meet the needs demanded of them.

Training in exponential understanding most likely will be needed. To ignore that fact is to play with disaster.

STEP TWO

[handwritten: How would we do this?]

The community college and university must develop a solid, continual research method, both formal and informal. Information and data will be critical to the leadership when making decisions on how to deal with changes upcoming from the technology. Since technologies are expected to develop exponentially, all possible data needs to be gathered before the development goes into rapid mode.

If that research is done successfully, then preparing for change as the velocity increases will be much more reasonable and accurate. In addition, it will put the institution in the most beneficial place to serve the technology or workforce needs.

STEP THREE

As the data and information are accumulated on the technologies involved, rapid, in-depth analysis will become critical. The community college and the university must be able to determine what their respective roles will be in dealing with the changes facing the institutions. This may entail additional personnel or retraining existing administrators.

STEP FOUR

Faculty and staff will need to be brought into the process. Lengthy meetings may be necessary to explain why the community college or university is so involved with technologies that are growing exponentially. Since this growth is so significantly different from a linear model, it may take some time to get the faculty and staff on board with the direction of the institution. The sooner an institution starts the relearning, updating process, the better position it will be in to deal with the impending technologies.

Further, faculty and staff could be very helpful as to researching formally or informally what the members are picking up on concerning the technology involved. Using all the internal resources possible will help keep the institution knowledgeable about the impact time frame of the technologies. The institution at all levels needs to be involved. Sitting on the beach unaware of the upcoming tsunami will only lead to failure.

STEP FIVE

All personnel in the college or university must understand why the institution is modifying its method of operation. It will be quite obvious to some, but not so much to others. Every member of the organization needs to know that the institution cannot be operated the way it was in the twentieth century. In order to keep the institution viable for all concerned, as technologies change, the institution will need to modify its operations.

For faculty and staff this may mean continuous retraining and reeducation to meet the needs of business, industry, and health organizations. The past is rapidly disappearing and the future comes with less warning than ever before. Everyone employed in the institution must be aware of why the changes are constantly being made.

CONCLUSION

The exponential executive will need to get used to dealing with continual, rapid change. It will become the new paradigm. It will demand everything the leader expected and more than was ever considered. It can be done, but will take a growth mind-set. The executives will be in Hannibal's situation; literally they will have to "find a way or make one." Either they are ready to deal with the technologies or the technologies will deal with them.

PREPARING FOR THE FUTURE

- To be successful in a world of serial disruptions, leaders must become exponential thinkers.
- Discarding the thinking of the past may be difficult, but will be critically important. Leaders will have to unlearn old habits and reeducate themselves for the new norm.

- Graduate programs will need to be seriously revised in order to be of assistance to future administrators.
- The importance of continual research will become absolutely critical.
- Faculty and staff will need to be continuously upgraded.
- For those who flourish in the exponential digital world, a mind-set of growth, rapid and continuous change will be mandatory.
- Dr. Carol Dweck of Sanford University is the guru of the growth mind-set.
- Although the future may look almost impossible, it may be helpful to recall the Carthaginian general, Hannibal Barca, who viewed the Alps with his soldiers and elephants behind him and was told going over the Alps was impossible. He is reported to have said, "We will find a way or make one."
- Business as usual in the status quo will not work in the exponentially developing digital world.
- A suggested method to deal with the rapidly changing future is the model ARPAC.
- The first step of the ARPAC method is awareness.
- It is critical that educational leaders become totally aware of the technological developments.
- The second step is continuous ongoing research.
- Both community colleges and universities should set up research committees to continually follow the development of specific technologies affecting their institutions.
- A vice president to coordinate research and reports of committees may become necessary.
- Regularly scheduled, periodic meetings of the entire faculty and staff to hear the reports of the research is critical.
- No longer can any educational institution wait and see what happens before deciding what to do. The institutions must be at the bleeding edge of knowledge on technological development.
- Today every college should be researching 3-D printing, autonomous vehicles, the Internet of Things, and genome development as they are all getting close to leaving linear development behind and moving to exponential development.
- The third step is analysis. Community college and university executives must be analytical and ready to plan future actions in a rapid, timely manner.

- Data will need to be analyzed to support leaders in making the right decisions in a timely manner.
- A data analysis committee could be the team that makes recommendations to the institution's leadership.
- The fourth step is action. Administrative leaders will need to make rapid, accurate decisions.
- Technology developing on the shaft of the hockey stick can in a blink of an eye turn everything into new pathways that the leadership must be aware of and ready to deal with.
- Leaders with a growth mind-set will have a chance of keeping up in remaining successful for all concerned.
- The fifth step is caring.
- Community college and university executives must care about the institution, its students, faculty/staff, the business community, and those in charge of local economic development.
- Awareness, research, planning, action, and caring all rest the foundation of a growth mind-set.
- The community college must remain well-informed on all upcoming changes.
- Community colleges may make extensive use of their Continuing Education Divisions to meet short-term training needs.
- No longer will the business world and the educational world be separate. If they are, it will invite disaster for all concerned.
- The university will need well-developed research into the business community to ascertain its needs.
- The five-step process is outlined to assist higher education leaders to keep their institutions viable and capable of dealing with the rapid change mode.
- The five steps include a learning process for administrators, solid and continual research, rapid in-depth analysis of data, faculty and staff kept updated, and transparency as to the change in operation.
- The community college will need to be continuously updated on the training needs of the local business community.
- The institution can make extensive use of its Continuing Education Division.
- The community college and the local business community must work together in a symbiotic manner for the success of all concerned.

- The university will be working on a higher level supporting the state and regional technology needs.
- It will work with business and health organizations.
- The Leadership Role is made up of five steps.
- Step One is to make certain the institution's leaders including president, vice presidents, deans, and department chairs are well aware of the impact of technologies on the institution.
- Step Two is to make certain that solid, continual research into the development of the technologies is going on and distributed on to all concerned.
- Step Three is analyzing the research to understand the development and impact of the technology involved on the institution.
- Step Four is bringing the faculty and staff into the process so that all employees of the institution understand the directions that are being taken and why.
- Step Five is sorting out what kinds of retraining and reeducation are needed for faculty and staff.
- The administrators working in an exponential environment need to get used to dealing with continual, rapid change.
- A growth mind-set is critical in all institutional leaders.
- Hannibal's statement, "We must find a way or make one," must become the mantra of the successful educational leader.

Chapter Eight

The Exponential
Institution of Higher Education

The exponential community college and university are just around the corner; they will be here in the very near future. The go-to-college, graduate, get-a-job, and hold the job for an entire career is disappearing rapidly. The go-to-college, get-a-job, go back to school to train for the next job, get the job, back to school to train for the next job, serial education, is beginning to become a reality.

SERIAL EDUCATION

As the serial method of education develops, it will change the way higher education is understood and will modify everything within it considerably. Students will come to the community college and university with totally different attitudes toward higher education. The Internet will make a great deal of information available for the interested student to become self-educated. MOOCs, still in the developing stage, may provide education to more students than ever before. Education by robot is already being experimented with in South Korea.

It would seem obvious that a great deal of the training and education in the future will be directly supportive of the technology involved. The business community will need employees who are digitally competent, who can deal with the technology. In addition, they will have the soft skills to work successfully with other employees.

Both technological competency and soft skills are becoming twin needs of the business community. The Information Technology (IT) department will no longer be a fiefdom unto itself. Students and employees will be highly competent in the technological world as well.

BUSINESS INTERESTS

Businesses will be constantly on the lookout for employees who can meet the technology needs of the business, adapt to rapid change, and work creatively with other humans and robots. The work world will become totally different from anything thought of as normal in the twentieth century (Ismail, 2014).

From the point of view of the student, training and education will become much more a student responsibility. The job a graduate is hired for today may be obsolete in a matter of months or a few years. Developing skills that can be used as a foundation for future positions in the workforce will become the norm. Learning to deal with the stress of what works today becoming obsolete in a relatively short period of time will become a significant part of the workforce environment.

DYNAMIC LEARNING CENTERS

The community college and university will become dynamic learning centers of information, data, and futuristic thinking that create pathways for students. Nothing will remain the same for long; most everything will change repeatedly and often, which means the administration, faculty, and staff of the institution will need to learn to work in a tumultuous environment at all times. They will have to adapt to what is coming next on a continual basis. Stress will play a part in the life and work of those employed in the institution at every level.

Rapid, continuous change most likely will be the norm for higher education during the twenty-first century, resulting from the exponentially developing technologies. The community college and the university will become the educational and training support in the ever-changing digital world.

APPRENTICESHIPS

Apprenticeships programs, which today are reappearing on the scene in a variety of occupations, should be recognized as a bridge to what is coming. If apprenticeships can keep up with the changes affecting the business community, they may be a workable response in the future as well. How long it will be able to meet the training needs of the future workforce remains to be seen.

Most likely more training and education will be needed, which can be obtained at the community college and university levels. Apprenticeships may provide the community college and university with a starting point in learning how to deal successfully with the continuously changing environment.

EDUCATION AND BUSINESS

The success of community colleges and universities in the future will require close partnerships with business and industry. The partnerships will help the institutions of higher education understand how the digital world is affecting the business world. They will assist institutions of higher education in keeping up to date with developments in technology that they can use to prepare for the education and training needed for the workforce of the future.

Lessons learned in the twentieth century with business/higher education working together will serve as an on-ramp to the technology superhighway needed as the two sectors symbiotically work closer together as never before. Major mergers between businesses and higher education could be a highway traveled extensively in the future.

ECONOMIC DEVELOPMENT

In addition, community colleges and universities need to work closely with economic development agencies. At the local level community colleges can be active in providing training for the workforce of new and developing business. At the regional, national, and international level, the universities can be active in developing the specific technologies that are needed in those areas. Standalone institutions of higher education will most likely decrease in number, perhaps disappear.

In addition, both the community college and the university will provide excellent support for new economic development opportunities on the local, state, and regional levels. It will not be unusual for a business to help identify the students in the community college for future employment at a particular or set of businesses.

The business may pay the tuition and fees of the students, supply the special equipment needed for training at the institution of higher education or the business itself. If an associate degree from a community college is not enough, that the institution could work directly with a university to offer a four-year degree at the community college, if that best serves the needs of the business who is looking for employees from the local area.

During the training and education, the student might work at the business about one third of the time, receiving pay as an employee. When the student graduated, he or she could go to work for the business for a period of time or go somewhere else to find employment, depending on the circumstances. It usually takes a reasonably large business or consortium of smaller businesses to serve in that capacity, but it is an excellent method for the student, the institution of higher education, and the business. A great deal more of that kind of symbiotic behavior will be seen in the future.

interesting insert

PERSONAL HEALTH

Leadership in higher education as well as faculty, staff, and students are going find themselves in a highly stressful environment as the exponentially developing technologies impact their lives and work. All will need to know the impact stress can put on their lives. It will be critical to their health and well-being that they take steps to make certain that they can appropriately deal with the digital environment in which they will live and work.

Students

The student will need to understand that making a living will require constant upgrading and retraining as the work changes as the result of software changes, working with robots, and the competition for the jobs that exist. That kind of continual change may take its toll and the student will need to be educated as to the best methods to deal with the stress it will cause.

Faculty

Faculty will need to understand that their positions will require serial upgrading and training to be able to serve the training and educational needs of the workforce. Rather than being hired for a full-time position in a particular discipline, faculty will find themselves more diversified in background and credentials to successfully be able to be retrained as needed. The need for continually upgrading and retraining in itself has the potential to increase the stress on the faculty member. They will also need to be educated as to the best methods in dealing with stress.

Staff

Staff, such as counselors, will need to be continually upgraded on how technologies are changing the world of work in order to be successful in directing students to the job du jour that needs a workforce. Career counseling will include in-depth explanations of how the working world operates. In short, such explanations would include getting trained and educated for a job that will change dramatically in a relatively short period of time, which will require coming back to school to learn what is needed for the next position.

Keeping up with the changes that are going on continually may be exciting, but it also has the potential to create stress. Counselors will need to be educated as to the best methods of dealing with stress. It is obvious that since all levels within the institutions of higher education will be dealing with continual stress, they will need to be dealt with through programs existing at the organization itself.

Leaders of community colleges and universities will need to be in a constant mode of re-learning how the world of work is modifying itself, often in very short periods of time. Jobs may literally be here today and gone tomorrow. Dealing with constant change will demand an extreme growth mind-set on the part of leaders. The pathway to the future will fork often and will come to dead ends as well as successes.

Wellness Centers

In the midst of this ever-changing environment, community college and university leaders, faculty, and staff will need to determine how to keep themselves healthy in the swirling environment in which they live and work. Wellness centers will become another standard feature of the institution. Everyone involved will need to find ways to keep themselves healthy and strong, physically and mentally.

Today the importance of regular workouts, yoga, and healthy eating is well known. However, that knowledge may not always be used to the greatest advantage. In the whirlwind of the digital world, these habits will become much more important to each individual. Most likely other activities will be added to the list of keeping one's health in excellent condition in the future. Perhaps employment may be divided into periods of work and rest on a daily or weekly basis.

Medications

There are already medications that help to stimulate the mind and body and those that cause relaxation. Perhaps the future will find humans becoming more dependent on drugs than they are now. It is a possible pathway of dealing with the stress of the digital age. On the other hand, humans may become cyborgs that use various digital devises placed on or in the body that help with stress and the speed of change. The future will tell.

The point is that a confluence of rapidly developing technologies will directly affect human beings that may or may not be healthful. Dealing with that situation will become critically important to the members of the workforce, the business community, and the higher education institutions. It is important that realistic, positive approaches to the digital future for human beings be formulated and developed. A proactive approach is necessary.

The transformation to digital education will create stressful situations throughout the institution to begin with. The serial education that will increase the stress levels for administrators, faculty, staff, and the students. Courses in stress management, wellness centers, and additional counselors will be needed. The future is just around the corner and higher education needs to be ready for its appearance.

CONCLUSION

The successful community colleges and universities in the digital world will be those which are aware, well-researched, and active in developing courses, certificates, and programs that meet the needs of businesses, which are developing as a result of exponential technologies. In addition, they will be prepared to assist all concerned to deal with the stress felt at all levels in the institutions.

PREPARING FOR THE FUTURE

- Serial education for students will become the new norm.
- Training and education in the future will directly support the technology involved.
- The business community will be searching for employees who can adapt to rapid change and work creatively with robots and humans.
- Much of the training and education will become much more a student responsibility.
- As things change repeatedly, the community college and university will become dynamic learning centers.
- Apprenticeship programs may serve as a bridge to the changing digital world.
- Partnerships between education and business will be critical.
- Community colleges and universities will need to work closely with economic development agencies in order to understand what may be coming in the near future.
- Businesses may be willing to pay the tuition and fees of students and supply any special equipment needed for training at the institution of higher education or at the business itself.
- Symbiotic behavior between education and business will flourish.
- Students will need to understand that making a living will require constant upgrading and retraining.
- Faculty will need to understand that their positions will require serial upgrading and training.
- Staff, such as counselors, will need to be continually upgraded on how technologies are changing the world of work.

- Leaders of community colleges and universities will need to be in a constant mode of relearning how the world of work is modifying itself.
- Wellness centers most likely will become a standard feature of every institution.
- Medications may help to stimulate the mind and body and cause relaxation. This could be a dangerous pathway to pursue.
- Stress management, wellness centers, and additional counselors will most likely be needed in higher education institutions to deal with the stress experienced by faculty, staff, and students.
- Successful community colleges and universities will be those who are well prepared to deal with the changes created by the digital world.

Chapter Nine

Projections

A big question is, "When are these exponential technologies going to appear?" To start with, all ten discussed in this book already exist in some form in 2019. They are developing somewhere along the blade of the metaphorical hockey stick. In general, it is safe to assume that all of them, with the possible exception of quantum computing and nanotechnology, will be fully operational by 2050, a little over 30 years from the publication of this book.

Many are already in the beginning stages of implementation such as 3-D printing, autonomous vehicles, genome development, personal robots, the Internet of Things, Bitcoin/Blockchain, and narrow artificial intelligence. Think of them as existing on the blade of the metaphorical hockey stick heading for the shaft, some closer than others. Farther back on the blade are nanotechnology, quantum computing, artificial general intelligence (AGI), and artificial super intelligence (ASI).

SHORT-TERM TECHNOLOGICAL DEVELOPMENT

3-D Printing: Additive Manufacturing

3-D printing currently exists in three distinct categories: manufacturing, health, and consumer products (Schwab, 2016). More could be on the way in the future as this technology is still in the beginning stages of development. Manufacturing businesses are already successfully experimenting with Additive Manufacturing constructing specific parts for automobiles, aircraft, and various types of machines (Barnatt, 2016). The biggest current issue is the length of time the layering process takes to make something. That will change in the near future and when it does, up the shaft 3-D will go.

Since 3-D printers are relatively inexpensive, many public schools, community colleges, and universities already have various types of 3-D printing onsite. The manufacturing versions of 3-D printing can be seen in small objects, both simple and very complicated in the educational arena.

At present, the development of this technology in the manufacturing area is slowed by the fact that a rapid method of layering has not yet be invented. However, as soon as rapid Additive Manufacturing is developed, it will make a tremendous impact on manufacturing in terms of precision, speed, and reduction of costs. By 2030, additive manufacturing will change current manufacturing processes on many fronts. By 2040, 3-D printing could take over much of the manufacturing industry throughout the world (Barnatt, 2016).

3-D Printing: Human Health

The second category, human health, may develop just as rapidly. Body parts from livers to lungs and more may become possible to construct from living tissue using the Additive Manufacturing process. Creating a specific body part for a particular human being will be the focus. The opportunity for this use of 3-D printing to escalate in the medical field is very possible as the demand already exists.

By 2030 successes in the production of body parts of all types may become an acceptable procedure for dealing with significant ailments that could be solved with a properly operating body part. By 2040, cyber-humans, individuals with various organs replaced, may become the norm (Barfield, 2015).

3D Printing: Consumer Products

Those who research future trends now believe that 3-D printing will soon enter the home environment in a big way. Consumers who need a particular part for the automobile, the clothes washer, or the toaster would be able to create the part needed. In other words, the potential for the home 3-D printer will most likely parallel the development and use of the personal computer as the cost per unit decreases and its ability to perform a variety tasks expands.

By 2030 it is estimated the home use for 3-D printing will be well on its way. Add another ten years and by 2040, the 3-D printer will be ubiquitous. How that will affect the lives of human beings worldwide is anyone's guess, but it will create a real change in what is now the domain of manufacturing businesses.

Autonomous Vehicles

The development of the autonomous vehicle is far along the blade of the metaphorical hockey stick. It is being tested by a number of organizations such as car manufacturers, the military, trucking businesses, Uber, Apple, Google, and others. It is approaching the shaft, about to move ahead at lightning speed. On the negative side, in March 2018 a woman crossing a street in Tempe, Arizona, was hit and killed by an autonomous car. The car had a safety driver person in the car, but the accident happened in spite of that safeguard.

That incident may slow the progress of the autonomous car, first, by resulting in fear on the part of the potential consumer and, second, by the creation of a new set of safety regulations developed by states and the federal government. However, that slowing of the progress will not stop the autonomous car and truck from becoming fully developed. Improved electronics and better computer algorithms used by the cars and trucks will soon appear and the pace will increase.

Since October 2017, refrigerators have been transported by autonomous trucks, with a safety driver, on the I-10 interstate highway for some 650 miles from El Paso, Texas, to Palm Springs, California (Davies, 2017). No accidents have taken place with that system of transportation yet. The Tesla car company has designed an entirely new autonomous truck that is receiving thorough testing.

By 2030, it is fully possible that autonomous cars will be riding on the streets and highways of the United States, Europe, and China. After Volvo was purchased by China, the car company stated it will produce all its automobiles powered by electric motors by the early 2020s. That could be a step toward producing cars and trucks that are wholly autonomous.

By 2040, approximately three million current truck drivers in the United States alone could be out of work permanently. That would mean a great number of displaced workers enrolling in community colleges and universities to gain the skills needed for a job in the digital world. On the other hand, autonomous cars will be a godsend to retirees who can no longer drive. They will be able to get around as they always have with a computer as the driver.

Genome Development: Humans

In 1953, Francis Crick and James Watson discovered the double helix of DNA, which over the years, led to a much better understanding of chemical processes in the human body (Crick, 1994).

> Since the turn of the century, the cost of sequencing an entire human genome has fallen by almost six orders of magnitude. The human genome project spent $2.7 billion to produce the first entire genome in 2003. By 2009 the cost per genome was down to $100K while today it is possible for researchers to pay a lab specializing in such matters only $1000 to sequence a human genome. (Schwab, 2016, p. 168)

In 2018, the cost to sequence a human genome dropped to less than $100. The reductions in cost were due to the increase of computer power generated according to Moore's law. The impact on human beings and agriculture is phenomenal. Thanks to a process titled Clustered Regularity Interspaced Short Palindromic Repeats (CRISPR) combined with an enzyme known as Cas9, CRISPR/Cas9, certain diseases will be cured, parents will be able to design the DNA of their children and new food processes will be created (Doudna et al., 2017).

By 2030, most likely many experiments will have been conducted with this new phenomenon. How controlled it will be by countries remains to be seen. By 2040 one can only assume that genetically planned children will be a fact of life, if not in the United States, then in other countries. Undoubtedly, there will be arguments over whether the possibility to design human beings should be done, but over time all opposition will most likely be overcome.

Genome Development: Agriculture

In the agricultural environment the ability to modify the genomes of plants and animals is already begun. Although for a couple of centuries agriculturalists have worked to change the DNA of plants and animals through the long term, tedious processes of breeding, today the change in DNA can be made in a matter of minutes. Adding muscle or fat to an animal or deleting possible diseases that have plagued them is now a reality that is just beginning (Doudna, 2017).

By 2030 new versions of fruits and vegetables or improved types of pork or beef will be in the grocery store. The changes may add days or weeks to fruits and vegetables before they spoil, which could be of great value to everyone. Research will have to be done to see if the revised DNA in the fruits and vegetables have any undesirable side effects on those consuming them. In the animal industry the growth rate may be vastly increased and meat produced that is more tender with less gristle, or whatever the desire du jour of the consumer may be.

By 2040 enough experimentation will have taken place for scientists to learn what works best and what should be discarded in the food sold to consumers. There could be tremendous improvement in amount food that could be grown in desert climates so that the Sahara may become an agricultural bonanza in the future. Scientists may determine how to increase growth rates in extreme cold environments as well. The possibilities appear endless.

Personal Robots

At present in the United States, personal robots are still mostly a Hollywood phenomenon. Robots of various sizes and shapes were used in science fiction films for many decades. A few were friendly, others were depicted in an adversarial disposition. Today a popular personal robot is the Roomba Robot, a vacuum cleaner that moves around the interior floor of the home. Beyond that device and Siri and Alexa, Americans are only beginning to see the need for personal robots as yet.

In Japan the situation is very different. The Japanese leaders understood the country was facing a problem with care for its elderly population. So they set about finding a solution. As early as 2005, Honda and other businesses in

Japan began developing personal robots with the aim of using them as direct care beings to work with the aging population. Moore's law in the computer field continued to develop exponentially. Although the early version of the Japanese robots were quite limited in what they could perform, as the years went by, their abilities increased significantly. By 2018, the Japanese had developed a variety of personal robots who look and act very much like real human beings.

In addition to the Japanese, the South Koreans, with support from Samsung, have developed an amazing array of personal robots. Many were seen working at the 2018 Winter Olympics in that country. China and some European countries are on the personal robot bandwagon as well. In the United States, the military is probably the most advanced in the personal robot field.

By 2030, personal robots will continue to be developed in almost all developed countries as it will be to their advantage. Already most countries developing personal robots have found that as long as the robots perform functions that are useful to human beings and if the robots look, talk, listen, and emotionally react as a human being would and function accurately, humans will tend to accept them rather easily. By 2030, most likely developers of personal robots will attempt to make them appear very humanlike so that they will be accepted by the consumer. That is already under way in Japan.

It is estimated that by 2040 most homes in developed countries will have personal robots in the home doing a variety of functions (Ford, 2015). By that point robots should be able to take care of housecleaning, cooking, ordering food, and doing minor maintenance chores. By 2050 most likely households will wonder how they ever did without a personal robot. Children will have grown up with them and will think of them as friends and associates.

The Internet of Things

The Internet of Things (IoT) already exists and is moving well along the blade of the metaphorical hockey stick toward the shaft. It is happening without much fanfare or public announcement, although if one is watching, it can be seen that the Spectrum cable company is already talking about it in its commercials.

National research organizations forecast that by 2020 somewhere be-tween 26 billion to 212 billion things will be transmitting information to the Internet and on to the cloud (Miller, 2015). By 2025 the number of things sending information to the cloud is expected to reach one trillion (Schwab, 2016). Who will use all this collected and stored information? Manufacturers, retailers, consumers, the products themselves, and ideas not yet imagined.

As with other technologies there will be positive and negative results. On the positive side, IoT could help companies work more effectively together; countries could more easily cooperate with each other; medical doctors could treat patients anywhere in the world; agricultural output could be increased globally, and a better understanding of the climate internationally could take place, to name a few things (Miller, 2015).

On the negative side, the more devices that connected on the IoT, the more points of entry there are for hackers who wish to do mischief or gain monetarily through manipulating the data. For the individual, unfor-tunately, privacy takes a back seat (Miller, 2015). More can be learned about the individual than ever, including the food consumed, the home energy used, the clothing worn, steps taken in a day, where a car is driven, or how much fruit is in the refrigerator. There appears to be no end to it.

By 2030 expect to see the IoT to have expanded into multiple trillions and become a huge enterprise in its own right for use by business, govern-ment, individuals, the medical field, agriculture, and the like. By 2040 the IoT will be as normal and useful as the Internet is today. The adjustment of humans to its existence will be completed.

Bitcoin/Blockchain

Bitcoin/Blockchain, an alternative financial system based in the digital world, has the potential to replace banks, financial systems, currency, and record keeping of financial and other transactions. The Bitcoin/Block-chain system has already been used by individuals, some legally, some questionably, to transmit funds through the system. The integrity of the system is ensured through heavy-duty cryptography. There is no bank or country involved in the transactions.

By 2030, some form of digital currency and transaction method most likely will be in existence. How well it will be secured and received by that time is anyone's guess. At present, there are a number of issues using Blockchain technology, such as security concerns, no centralized control, cost, lack of scalability, lack of regulation, and hype (Gates, 2017). These issues will have to be corrected before the Bitcoin/Blockchain type of financial system will be accepted universally. Most likely that can happen; time will tell.

By 2040, either the problems surrounding the digital currency will have been solved and the process used, or the process will be no longer in existence. From the perspective of today, it is hard to tell what the potential for a digital currency will be. However, this technology, like the others existing in the early twenty-first century, may continue to exist and have an impact on daily lives.

Narrow Artificial Intelligence

Narrow Artificial intelligence and machine learning already exist and have been used on numerous occasions. One example is IBM's Deep Blue supercomputer, which in 1997 won over the world's champion chess player Gary Kasparov (Kasparov, 2017). Some years later in 2011, IBM's Watson computer was able to beat two of the *Jeopardy*'s all-time champions, Ken Jennings and Brad Rutter (Baker, 2011). Although these two computers were able to overcome champions in two different fields, one in chess and the other in a game show, neither were programmed to do much more.

However, narrow AI is the beginning of a development that could lead to artificial general intelligence (AGI). Narrow AI is a kind of practice environment for learning how the computer can be developed to the point where it is as capable as the human brain. That is not going to happen tomorrow, but it is predicted to be possible by 2045 (Kurzweil, 2005). Previous to the actuality of AGI, be on the lookout for an increasing number of narrow AIs coming on the scene.

By 2030 the sheer number of different uses of narrow AI will grow in numbers and abilities. The business world, government, the medical field, and others will use of narrow AI for almost anything imaginable. By 2040, the amount of experience with narrow AI and the continued 18-month doubling of computer power and storage will lead to the next step in computer evolution, AGI, which will bring the computer to the point where it is equal in mental ability to the human being.

LONG-TERM TECHNOLOGICAL DEVELOPMENT

Nanotechnology

Entering the world of nanotechnology opens the door to the quantum world which is totally different from what is experienced as a human being on a day-to-day basis. Whereas the observable world basically follows Newton's laws, the nanotechnology world throws those well-known axioms out the window. Nanotechnology exists in the quantum world, where what makes sense to humans on a daily basis does not exist.

Although a lot of fanfare was heard when nanotechnology was first presented, not as much actually developed since the late 1980s as was expected. That does not mean the possibilities do not exist; it simply means that working at the level of atoms was much more difficult and dangerous than what originally might have been thought.

With that in mind, what can be expected by 2030? Probably some small developments, unless the major obstacles can be overcome. More research and experimentation will be needed to move nanotechnology ahead. By 2040, with breakthroughs, it may be possible to manufacture objects starting at the atom level. However, it may take until the end of the century for nanotechnology to become a common phenomenon.

Quantum Computing

As was stated in the comments on nanotechnology, the quantum world is very different from the observable world. Quantum computing exists in that environment. To begin with, scientists have discovered that in the quantum world atoms exist in two places at once. That was not a concept easily accepted even by Albert Einstein (Kisak, 2016). However, over the decades, twentieth-century scientists proved it to be true. Nothing in the observable world and universe exists in two places at once according to the five human senses; so it is hard for non-scientists to envision such a phenomenon.

Quantum computing is moving along the blade of the metaphorical hockey stick with persistent speed toward the shaft. Billions of dollars are being spent globally to obtain the quantum computer. Compare this early model quantum computer to the Commodore computer of the 1970s. It does work, but is very limited.

By 2030 it is possible that the Chinese could have an operational quantum computer with considerable power. D-Wave, a company in Canada, has developed an expanded, but limited version already (Kisak, 2016). Perhaps U.S. and European universities will not be far behind. Being first in the world to successfully develop this technology is very important because the quantum computer could make most other computers obsolete overnight.

By 2040, if both China and the United States along with its European allies are on about the same footing with quantum computing, the world could change at speeds never before imagined. By 2045, the Singularity, a computer as intelligent as a human being, could become reality. With quantum computer power, Artificial Super Intelligence (ASI) could be in existence by the late 2040s.

Artificial General Intelligence (AGI)

With intense research those technologies farther back on the hockey stick blade could move toward the shaft more quickly. Ray Kurzweil (2005), author of *The Singularity Is Near*, estimates that if the doubling of classical computer power continues to take place every 18 months, a form of artificial general intelligence (AGI) is possible by 2045. In other words, Kurzweil can envision the possibility of an extremely powerful computer that could equal the brain power in all respects of a human being by that date.

Of course, he could be wrong; it might happen earlier than 2045 with quantum computing power, or it might take longer. However, no matter which futurist is researched, all fully expect that artificial general intelligence will exist by 2100 (Barrat, 2013). In fact, most prognosticate that the computer will be far beyond AGI by the end of the twenty-first century. Most believe that a computer with artificial super intelligence (ASI) will exist by then.

Does one need to worry about a computer with ASI capabilities? By itself, maybe not. Connect the existing computer power and the cloud that will exist by 2045 to a robot(s), then one should worry a lot. An ASI could develop an IQ of a million or more, which would give it mental power far beyond any human being who ever existed. What would a computer connected to robots do to the world as it currently exists? Stop and think about that unthinkable situation for a moment.

An ASI could develop a phenomenally positive environment for human beings; on the other hand, it could make humans its slaves, or, worse yet, it could eliminate *homo sapiens* altogether (Barrat, 2013). There is no way to know for sure today. Since humans are creating the possibility of an ASI in the future, if things go well humans will take the credit. If things go bad, humans may no longer exist.

For the pessimists, consult *Our Final Invention: Artificial Intelligence and the End of the Human Era*, by James Barrat (2013). For the optimists, try Woodrow Barfield (2015), *Cyber-Humans: Our Future with Machines*. For the independents, become aware, research all technologies and prepare to take action.

CONCLUSION

Getting some idea of when the various technologies may appear must be a continual process of the leaders of higher education. Waiting to see what happens will not work. Letting someone else look after it will not work. Ignoring it in hopes it will go away will not work. Awareness, research, planning, action, and caring will give the leaders of higher education a shot at dealing positively with what is to come. Hopefully together they can state with Hannibal, "we must find a way or make one" as they climb up the mountain range of digital uncertainty and make their way down the other side to success.

PREPARING FOR THE FUTURE

- The 10 technologies discussed in this book are at different stages of development.
- 3-D printing currently exists in three distinct categories: manufacturing, health, and consumer products.
- As soon as the layering process is speeded up, 3-D printing will come into its own.
- Many public schools, community colleges, and universities already have various types of 3-D printing on site.
- By 2040 3-D printing could take over much of the manufacturing industry throughout the world.

- 3-D printing of human organs is currently under development. By 2040 individuals may have various organs replaced.
- 3-D printing is expected to enter the home environment in the near future. By 2040 3-D printing should be ubiquitous and may be as normal as a PC.
- Autonomous vehicles are developing rapidly. Governmental regulation will slow it down to some degree.
- Many countries including the United States, those in Europe, and China are working on autonomous automobiles.
- Autonomous trucks could negatively affect truck driving as a way of making a living. By 2040 many of the current 3 million truck drivers could be out of work.
- The sequencing of the human genome has dropped to less than $100 per person.
- CRISPR/Cas9, which will allow for genome modification, may help to cure certain diseases. In addition, parents may be able to design the DNA of their children.
- But by 2040 genetically planned children could be in existence, if not in the United States, then in other countries.
- Genome modification in plants and animals is ongoing and well possibly could cure a number of chronic diseases in animals in the near future.
- By 2040 sufficient experimentation should have taken place for scientists to learn what works best and what should be discarded in food modification.
- The development of personal robots in Japan has been going on since 2005.
- The Japanese are developing a variety of personal robots that look and act very much like real human beings.
- By 2040 many homes in developed countries may have personal robots to do a variety of functions.
- Children who grew up with personal robots in the house will most likely think of them as friends or associates.
- By 2025 the Internet of Things will be sending information to the cloud at an expected rate of one trillion annually.
- By 2040 the Internet of Things will be as normal and useful as the Internet is today.

- The Bitcoin/Blockchain financial process, although having security problems, will most likely solve them by 2030.
- If not, the process may be no longer in existence by 2040.
- Narrow artificial intelligence such as Deep Blue or Watson will continue to develop in other areas.
- Narrow AI is a kind of practice environment for learning how the computer can be developed to the point where it is as capable as the human brain.
- By 2045 it is prognosticated that artificial general intelligence will exist.
- Nanotechnology is in existence but operates in the quantum world.
- Nanotechnology is developing rather slowly because working at the level of atoms is extremely difficult and dangerous.
- By 2040 it may be possible to manufacture objects using atoms.
- Quantum computing is moving ahead steadily with companies in the United States, Canada, and Europe.
- China is going all out in the quantum world.
- If quantum computing is developed before 2045, the Singularity, a computer as intelligent as a human being, could become reality before 2045.
- Artificial general intelligence, expected to be in existence by 2045, brings with it great hope for technological breakthroughs and great fear of negative effects on human beings.
- Cyber-humans may be one way to deal successfully with an artificial general intelligence.
- We, like Hannibal Barca, will need to "find a way or make one" to be successful in the future.

Chapter Ten

Mission and Vision

MISSION

Community colleges and universities usually developed the missions for their institutions when they were created. Modifications were made periodically, perhaps in connection with re-accreditation or some other significant event. A few community colleges and universities may have made changes in their missions annually.

However, for the most part, once an acceptable mission was written for an institution, it tended to continue on for years, as if it were chipped in stone. As long as students were properly educated, the business community appropriately provided with training, and the economic development agencies supported, things moved along successfully.

VISION

The vision for the community college or university pretty much followed the track of the mission with changes usually required by significant modifications of programs or the re-accreditation process. However, the vision was also looked upon as something that could be changed more frequently. Modifications to the vision might be made with the hiring of a new president who determined that different directions for the institution were in the best interest of the student, the college, the business community, and/or the economic development needs.

EFFECT OF TECHNOLOGIES

What community colleges and universities face in the twenty-first century is something altogether different. The developing technologies will require that both types of institutions transform themselves rapidly to keep up with the changes the technologies will bring. In the very near future, 3-D printing, autonomous vehicles, the Internet of Things, genome development, and perhaps Bitcoin/Blockchain will directly affect program offerings.

Changes in programs or the development of new ones using twentieth-century processes might take a year or more to complete. The twenty-first-century technologies will demand a much faster decision-making process to initiate new courses, programs, and degrees. Exponential technologies will require exponential thinking and decision making. The community colleges traditionally have had a division of Continuing Education and/or Workforce where changes that were needed immediately could be addressed. That experience will prove useful for success in the twenty-first century.

REDEFINING THE MIDDLE CLASS

The development of technologies will have many side effects on the culture and society at large. It will cause the redefinition of the middle class in the United States. In the twentieth century the middle class developed as the manufacturing economy gradually replaced the agricultural economy. Individuals who left the farm for the city became the manufacturing workforce with higher incomes and improved living styles. This movement happened by providing the choice for a better life.

The developing technologies of the twenty-first century will delete many of what are thought to be good jobs today. Computers and robots will take over anywhere from 10 percent to 50 percent of current repetitive jobs (Schwab, 2018). As the agricultural society watched a change from farming to a manufacturing society in the 1900s, the twenty-first-century society will experience a transformation from a manufacturing-based workforce to a digital-based workforce. Unfortunately, this transformation of work will not be by choice. It will be required by the technologies.

SERIAL EDUCATION

The new middle class will be made up of individuals who have a strong educational background, a thorough understanding of the digital world, and a tenacious willingness to keep up with the developments of the technologies. There will be few other choices. The members of the workforce will be in a constant state of reeducating themselves. Just as the twentieth century saw the transition from working on the farm to working in the city upset society, so the twenty-first century will observe a transition from working in manufacturing to working in a digital world, with serial disruptions affecting society.

CHANGE IN MISSION AND VISION

The mission and vision of the community college and the university will need revision often and dramatically if the institutions desire to remain viable and successful. Sitting back and waiting to see what happens will be the mantra of failure. Looking ahead with a future-focused, growth mind-set will become the norm of successful leaders of higher education.

CONCLUSION

The community college and university will need to prepare for an ever-changing world of technology. The mission and vision of higher education institutions will need to be modified and redesigned repeatedly to meet the needs of the twenty-first-century technologies, which in turn have the potential of creating more phenomenal changes in the world of work and the living standards of all concerned.

Community colleges and universities will play a much greater role in helping students to understand the changes the many technologies create on life and work. Getting a serial education will become critically important for all concerned. Community colleges and universities must be prepared for the onslaught of individuals who will need guidance, education, and understanding of what it means to be successful in life and work in the foreseeable future.

PREPARING FOR THE FUTURE

- The mission of community colleges and universities have lasted for long periods of time.
- The vision of higher education institutions are changed more often.
- The twenty-first-century technologies will demand a much faster decision-making process which may create changes in the college's mission and vision more often.
- The development of new technologies will cause the redefinition of the middle class in the United States.
- The workforce of the middle class will find itself in a constant state of reeducation.
- The mission and vision of higher education institutions will be modified and redesigned repeatedly to meet the needs of the twenty-first-century technologies.

Chapter Eleven

The Exponential
Graduate Program

When researching, writing, and thinking about the exponential effects that twenty-first-century technologies will have on community colleges and universities, it became obvious that a change on higher education leadership programs was needed. Although this book is focused on how two different types of higher education, community colleges and universities, need to transform themselves to remain viable in the near future, there is no doubt that more is needed.

The doctorate programs offered to educate individuals interested in becoming successful department heads, deans, vice presidents, provosts, and presidents need to be transformed as well. One of the themes of this book is that what worked well in leadership during the twentieth century will not bring success in the technology-riddled twenty-first. What better place to bring up the topic of the impact of technologies on community colleges and universities than in the graduate programs teaching prospective leaders in higher education?

In a doctoral program focused on higher education leadership, teaching students what worked well in the twentieth century and expecting it to lead to success in the twenty-first century is not going to work in the best interest of the teaching institutions or the graduate students soon to be taking on the mantle of leadership. The world of exponential change cannot be dealt with successfully using linear models. Linear approaches will lead to failure, which is not what graduate students want nor should the university involved be pursuing.

As a result, this chapter addresses what a doctoral program in educational leadership culminating in an EdD degree should include in the best interest of the university, the graduate students, and the future institutions the program's graduates are expected to lead successfully. To discuss this topic, the Community College Executive Leadership (CCEL) program at Wingate University in Charlotte, North Carolina, will be used as an example. The CCEL program at Wingate University is an EdD program. The degree focuses on what is needed to successfully lead a community college.

Wingate's EdD program was initiated in 2013. It was developed using a model from Vanderbilt University and included ideas from the Aspen Institute, Ferris State University, and other sources. The three-year CCEL program uses a cohort style for students and has a graduation rate of 85 percent. Classes are held on Saturdays from 9:00 am–5:00 pm with five class sessions scheduled for each course. In the fall and spring semesters two courses are offered and during the summer semester, three courses are taught, one of which is online. With the exception of the two online classes, all the other courses are taught in a traditional face-to-face manner at the Ballantyne Campus in Charlotte.

Until the summer session 2017, all courses in the program were taught using models emanating from the twentieth century. Although most of the texts were copyrighted in the twenty-first century, they were not focused on dealing with the impact of the technological changes emerging in this century. Prior to the summer of 2017 all courses were configured and developed along twentieth-century lines. Little attention was paid to the 10 technologies discussed in this book in any of the 14 didactic courses.

In the summer session of 2017, a change was made in the course titled the Community College in the 21st Century. That summer two texts were used: *The Coming Jobs War* by Jim Clifton, chairman of Gallup Poll, and *Rise of the Robots: Technology and the Threat of a Jobless Future* by Martin Ford, founder of a Silicon Valley–based software development firm. As it turned out, both books excited the students as they gave them a look into what the future might bring in particular to the job world. It was a real eye-opening experience for many of the students. The texts discussed issues that peaked their interest.

In the course, the students were divided into groups which were given a research project for the summer on one the following topics: artificial intelligence, personal robots, 3-D printing, autonomous vehicles and drones, genome development medical and agricultural, and nanotechnology. The students were told that if their research and written reports were of suitable quality, the professor would edit them and add four additional chapters on the Internet of Things, Bitcoin/Blockchain, quantum computing and exponential leadership. Further, their work would be submitted the work for publication. That promise stimulated student interest and excitement.

The upshot of their efforts for the course was a book titled *Facing an Exponential Future: Technology and the Community College*, published by Rowman and Littlefield in June 2018. If the students were excited while doing the research, it was nothing compared to their joy upon receiving a copy of the book with their names in it.

The book demonstrated that graduate students appeared to be interested in what was going to appear at their institutions during their leadership careers. Although the student interest was strong, it was not clear if it was a fluke, good luck, or a sincere reaction on the part of the students.

During the following spring semester of 2018 with a different group of students in a graduate course titled Comprehensive Planning and Program Evaluation, another text was added to the course titled, *The Fourth Industrial Revolution* by Klaus Schwab, executive chairman of the World Economic Forum. The students were asked to study the book, list 10 concepts they thought were important, and discuss what they thought community colleges reaction would be to those concepts. They were also asked to do some additional research on the topics cited in the text.

The students were divided into groups, each of which were assigned to teach a set of chapters from the book to the class. The professor expected a run-of-the-mill set of presentations, even though the book did a great job describing the technologies developing in the twenty-first century. Instead, the students were super excited and eager to present their ideas on the book and the additional research they had conducted.

Their enthusiasm for learning more about what might face them in the future as a community college leader supported the conclusion that they were extremely interested were in what the twenty-first century would bring to their institutions and how it would affect their future careers.

As a result, during the summer of 2018 the texts by Jim Clifton and Martin Ford were again used in the Community College in the 21st Century course. Both books went over very well with the students. The students were divided into groups and asked to research two specific topics and write a paper on each of the topics. Those topics included 3-D printing and the Internet of Things; autonomous vehicles and personal robots; nanotechnology and artificial intelligence; human and agricultural genome; and quantum computing and a future technology center.

The research was to include seven to twelve sources for each topic, which must include contacting two to four community colleges and universities that were already working on the topic area that group was pursuing to see where the institutions were in working with a specific technology. The students investigated community colleges and universities in North Carolina, South Carolina, Virginia, New York, Maine, and Ohio. Some went to actually visit the distant institutions at their own expense. That was not a requirement.

The class was informed that that their work would be edited, the professor would add chapters from his research, and every effort would be made to obtain publication of the resulting book. The students knew that the class before them had been successful in having their work published; consequently, they put in a significant effort during the summer course. Again the graduate students were phenomenally interested in how twenty-first-century technologies would affect their institutions and their own careers.

During the fall semester, *Facing an Exponential Future: Technology and the Community College*, was added to the Education Leadership course. This text generated considerable interest on the part of the new students in their first semester of Wingate's Community College Executive Leadership program.

Which leads to where does the program go from here? In the first two years of the CCEL program there are a total of 14 courses. The third year has two courses per semester on writing and researching their selected Capstone Project. The author's goal is to have at least one text on technology in each of the six courses that he teaches. If the texts meet with student success, the author plans to work with the other faculty in the program to see if they would be interested in refocusing a segment of their courses on the impact of technologies on community colleges and universities.

Since technologies will impact all the higher education divisions in the near future, they could easily be worked into many of the other courses. Here are some ideas as to which texts might work in these courses contained in CCEL.

- Managing Finance, Budget and Facilities (Tapscott's *Blockchain Revolution*)
- Organizational Development and Change (Kelly's *The Inevitable*)
- Information Management Systems (Miller's the *Internet of Things*)
- Teaching, Learning and Student Success (Aoun's *Robot Proof*)
- Community and Governmental Relations (Friedman's *Thank You for Being Late)*
- Presidents and Executive Leadership (Dweck's *Mindset*).

The goal behind bringing twenty-first-century technologies into most of the courses in the program would be to focus student thinking on what will face them in their future careers as administrators. Better to learn about them now and be prepared, then to learn about them later when exponential change suddenly appears at the doorstep of their institutions. Dealing with surprises are often the most difficult situations. Having an awareness of what is coming allows one to be prepared.

It is incumbent on all current leaders in community colleges and universities to become aware, informed, and prepared for the technological situations that they are going to face in the near future. Exponentially developing technologies, if one is not aware of their existence, seem to appear from nowhere. They will make the lives and careers of administrators most difficult as they try to catch up with a phenomenon that seems to have no end of energy.

It is clear that much work needs to be done at the university level to prepare community college and university leaders to be able to deal successfully with the technologies that are up and coming in the near future. That is not to talk about the big three: artificial intelligence, nanotechnology, and quantum computing. Maybe it will take cyber-humans to deal successfully with those technologies by 2050 (Barfield, 2015).

The revision of higher education leadership programs will be required in a matter of a few years. Without program transformation to deal with the technological changes on the horizon, the university leadership programs are headed down a path leading to mediocrity, both on the part of the institution and those being taught. Those involved in graduate leadership programs will need to understand the Awareness, Research, Planning, Action, Caring (ARPAC) process method of dealing with the twenty-first-century technologies, which is discussed in chapter 7.

Using ARPAC to revise the current program being offered will help those universities revise their graduate leadership programs to bring the technologies of the current century into the classroom. That is critical for the graduate students who will soon be expected to take on leadership positions in higher education. They must be well aware of what they will soon face as leaders.

CONCLUSION

It seems clear that educational leadership programs should be strongly considering adding texts or research projects on the impact of technologies on teaching and learning in the twenty-first century. The students now in elementary and secondary school will be experiencing those technologies and will soon be enrolling in higher education to make sense of it. It is critical that those leading institutions of higher education be knowledgeable of the disruptive results and how to deal with them.

PREPARING FOR THE FUTURE

- Changes are needed in higher education leadership programs to include the study of technologies that will impact higher education.
- Wingate University's Community College Executive Leadership EdD program was developed from a Vanderbilt University model with input from the Aspen Institute, Ferris State University, and other sources.
- The courses were configured and developed along twentieth-century leadership models.
- In 2017 one course delved into the impact of 10 technologies on community colleges.
- A book titled, *Facing an Exponential Future: Technology and the Community College*, published in June 2018 by Rowman and Littlefield, resulted from the students' work.
- The concept of investigating the impact of technologies on community colleges was further investigated in two more courses.
- Plans are to place an appropriate text on technology in each of six courses taught by the author.

- Suggested possible texts for other courses in the program are listed.
- It is incumbent that courses in higher education leadership include a text or information on the ten technologies discussed in this book.
- The awareness, research, planning, action, caring process has the potential to assist future leaders in higher education as they find themselves being impacted by technologies in the twenty-first century.

Chapter Twelve

Future Technology Center

There is one more thing that community college and university leaders may want to consider. Since the readers of this book are now aware to some degree of the ten technologies discussed in this book, some may wish to take immediate action rather than wait around for the results from further research. Maybe some entrepreneurial institutions may want to forge ahead and become part of the development of the technologies. Why wait? Why not help develop what is to come?

A possible method is to initiate a Future Technology Center, a place where three things can happen. First, students can experiment with possibilities using the latest in teaching technologies. Second, the local business community could use the center to learn about the latest developments in their areas of interest. Third, the center, which has the latest in equipment for the given technology, can produce the actual parts needed by the business for a price. The business leaders are happy because they can obtain the item immediately and are willing to pay for it, which brings in revenue to the center and the ultimately to the institution.

Florence Darlington Technical College in Florence, South Carolina, has jumped into the fray and initiated such a center, the Southeastern Institute of Manufacturing and Technology (SiMT). This center houses a number of technologies included 3-D printing and 3-D virtual reality for training in the technical and health fields, to name a couple.

The idea would be to develop a center that would serve not only the students of the college, but just as importantly, the businesses in the service area of the college. Beyond that, the center could serve manufacturing needs of the region or more. The SiMT supports the college academically with the latest in technology and produces revenue over expenses that help support the college financially. It is a method of keeping up with the latest in technology while providing an alternative revenue stream for the college.

Something like the SiMT could be developed at any community college or university. It could be financed and owned by the foundation so that it does not interfere in any way with the policies and procedures governing the state finances. A few community colleges have done something like this in the past. It has great potential for the institution involved to attain as much self-sufficiency as possible.

Something to consider.

Epilogue

I have been involved with education my entire career, the first three years in public schools teaching seventh and eighth grade English. After that, I became part of the community college movement as a faculty member, department chair, dean, vice president, and president. I also served as a system president before I initially retired. I have always believed in education to help people get ahead in the world and live happy, productive lives.

I soon found that retirement was not to my liking. About a year later, I began my current work as a professor in a university at the graduate level. I work with students who are interested in becoming community college and university administrators. In making an attempt to guide those who will lead our institutions of higher education though the upcoming decades, I decided to research what the higher education will face in the next three decades.

That research resulted in two books, *Facing and Exponential Future: Technology and the Community College* (2018) and *Exponential Technologies: Higher Education in an Era of Serial Disruptions* (2019). I plan to follow these with another which will demonstrate what community colleges and universities are currently doing to deal with the technologies in the twenty-first century.

I have always been an optimist and see no reason to change now; however, what I found in my research about technologies that will face us in the future is enough to make me step back. Although the future appears a bit frightening, I will continue on with the best intentions of supporting others and teaching, that although the future may look different, there are always possibilities we cannot envision that bring us to new places we had overlooked or did not imagine.

I end this book with a statement by Hannibal Barca, who when standing in front of the Swiss Alps with 50,000 men and 37 elephants behind him, looked at the mountain range with a narrow trail going up. He was told getting up and over that mountain was impossible. After some consideration, Hannibal is recorded to have said, "We will find a way or make one." Within 15 days, he led his men over the mountain to the plains on the other side.

In the darkest hours, if such appear in the future, let Hannibal's statement be our guide: "We will find a way or make one."

References

Aoun, J. (2017). Robot-proof: Higher education in the age of artificial intelligence. Cambridge, MA: The MIT Press.

Baker, S. (2011). *Final Jeopardy: Man vs. machine and the quest to know everything.* New York: Houghton Mifflin Harcourt.

Barfield, W. (2015). *Cyber-humans: Our future with machines.* New York: Springer International Publishing.

Barnatt, C. (2016). *3-D printing.* Third Edition. ExplainingTheFuture.com.

Barrat, J. (2013). *Our final invention: Artificial intelligence and the end of the human era.* New York: St. Martin's Press.

Clifton, J. (2011). *The coming jobs war: What every leader must know about the future of job creation.* New York: The Gallup Press.

Cohen, A.M., Brawer, F.B., & Kisker, C.B. (2014). *The American community college.* San Francisco: Jossey Bass.

Crick, F. (1994). *The astonishing hypothesis: The scientific search for the soul.* New York: Charles Scribner's Sons.

Davies, A. (2017). *Self-driving trucks are now delivering refrigerators. Wired. com.* https://www.wired.com/story/embark-self-driving-truck-deliveries/.

Doudna, J.A. & Sternberg, S.H. (2017). *A crack in creation: Gene editing and the unthinkable power to control evolution.* New York: Houghton Mifflin Harcourt.

Drexler, K. E. (1987). *Engines of creation: The coming era of nanotechnology.* New York: Anchor Books, published by Doubleday.

Dweck, C.S. (2006). *Mindset: The new psychology of success.* New York: Ballantine Books.

Fingas, J. (2017). *IBM squeezes 30 billion transistors into a fingernail-sized chip. engadget.com.* https://www.engadget.com/2017/06/05/ibm-5nm-chip -manufacturing/.

Ford, M. (2015). *Rise of the robots: Technology and the threat of a jobless future.* New York: Basic Books.

Friedman, T.L. (2016). *Thank you for being late: An optimist's guide to thriving in the age of accelerations.* New York: Farrar, Straus, and Giroux.

Gates, Mark. (2017). *Blockchain: Ultimate guide to understanding blockchain, bitcoin, cryptocurrencies, smart contracts, and the future of money.*

Greengard, S. (2015). *The Internet of Things.* Cambridge, MA: The MIT Press Essential Knowledge Series.

Hawkins, A. (2018). *Waymo's self-driving trucks will start delivering freight in Atlanta. TheVerge.com,* https://www.theverge.com/2018/3/9/17100518/waymo-self-driving-truck-google-atlanta.

Hyacinth, B. (2017). *The future of leadership: Rise of automation, robotics and artificial intelligence.*

Hyatt, K., and Paukert C. (2018). *Self-Driving cars: A level-by-level explainer of autonomous vehicles.* Road/Show by CNET.

Ismail, S. (2014). *Exponential organizations: Why new organizations are ten times better, faster, and cheaper than yours (and what you can do about it).* New York: Diversion Books.

Kasparov, G. (2017). *Deep thinking: Where machine intelligence ends and human creativity begins.* New York: Perseus Books, LLC.

Kelly, K. (2016). *The inevitable: Understanding the 12 technological forces that will shape our future.* New York: Viking.

Kisak, P.F. (Ed.). (2016). *An overview of quantum computing: The state of the art in computers.*

Kurzweil, R. (2005). *The Singularity is near.* London: Penguin Books.

Lancel, S. (1998) *Hannibal.* Malden, MA: Blackwell Publishers, Inc.

Lin, J. & Singer, P.W. (October 10, 2017). *China is opening a new quantum research supercenter. Popular Science.*

Miester, J.C. & Mulcahy, K.J. (2017). *The future workplace experience: 10 rules for mastering disruption in recruiting and engaging employees.* New York: McGraw Hill Education.

Miller, M. (2015). *The internet of things: How smart TVs, smart cars, smart homes, and smart cities are changing the world.* Indianapolis: Que Publishing.

Morgan, J. (2014). *The future of work: Attract new talent, build better leaders, and create a competitive organization.* Hoboken, NJ: John Wiley and Sons.

SAE International (2016).

Schwab, K. (2016). *The fourth industrial revolution.* Geneva, Switzerland: World Economic Forum.

Schwab, K., & Davis, N. (2018). *Shaping the fourth industrial revolution.* Geneva, Switzerland: World Economic Forum.

Scientific American Editors (Ed.) (2002). *Understanding nanotechnology*. New York: Warner Books, Inc.

Tapscott, D. & Tapscott, A. (2016). *Blockchain revolution: How the technology behind bitcoin is changing money, business, and the world*. New York: Penguin Random House.

West, D. (2018). *The future of work: Robots, AI and automation*. Washington, DC: The Brookings Institution.

Witt, A.A., Wattenbarger, J.L., Gollattscheck, J.F., & Suppiger, J.E. (1994). *America's community colleges: The first century*. Washington, DC: Community College Press.

About the Author

Darrel W. Staat served as president at two technical colleges in Maine, one community college in Virginia, and the South Carolina Technical College System. Currently, he is the coordinator and professor of an EdD program in community college administration at Wingate University, Ballantyne Campus in Charlotte, North Carolina.

hockey stick analogy